stress:
A Brief History

Blackwell Brief Histories of Psychology

The *Blackwell Brief Histories of Psychology* offer concise, accessible, and lively accounts of key topics within psychology, such as emotion, intelligence, and stress, that have had a profound effect on psychological and cultural life. The books in this series provide a rich sense of historical context while remaining grounded in contemporary issues and research that will be of interest to both academic and general readers.

Stress: A Brief History
Cary Cooper and Philip Dewe

Evolutionary Thought in Psychology: A Brief History
Henry Plotkin

Emotions: A Brief History
Keith Oatley

Intelligence: A Brief History
Robert J. Sternberg and Anna T. Cianciolo

stress

A Brief History

**CARY L. COOPER
AND PHILIP DEWE**

Blackwell
Publishing

350 Main Street, Malden, MA 02148-5020, USA
108 Cowley Road, Oxford OX4 1JF, UK
550 Swanston Street, Carlton, Victoria 3053, Australia

First published 2004 by Blackwell Publishing Ltd

Library of Congress Cataloging-in-Publication Data

Cooper, Cary L.
Stress: A brief history / Cary L. Cooper and Philip Dewe.—1st ed.
p. cm.—(Blackwell brief histories of psychology; 1)
Includes bibliographical references and index.
ISBN 1–4051–0744–8 (alk. paper)—ISBN 1–4051–0745–6 (pbk : alk. paper)
1. Stress (Psychology)—Research—Methodology—History. I. Dewe,
Philip. II Title. III. Series.

BF575.S75C646 2004
155.9′042′09 — dc22
2003023501

A catalogue record for this title is available from the British Library.

Set in 10/12pt Book Antique
by Kolam Information Services Pvt. Ltd, Pondicherry, India
Printed and bound in the United Kingdom
by TJ International, Padstow, Cornwall

For further information on
Blackwell Publishing, visit our website:
http://www.blackwellpublishing.com

To Rachel Davies Cooper and Linda Trenberth

Contents

Acknowledgments

When we began this brief history of stress we had a plan. What we should have guessed, as "lay historians," is that history doesn't always work to a plan. We were soon being led by events and personalities as the history of stress, as we saw it, began to unfold. What we have written reflects our view of the history of stress. That is why the book is tilted "A Brief History of Stress." It should not be regarded as *the* history of stress as we, like others before us, were continually faced with the dilemma of what to include, what events were significant, how to capture shifts in focus, and how to order things so that they illustrated the debates, discussion, and controversy that accompanies a topic like stress. We also wanted to avoid sequencing events and issues in a way that made it seem as if there was some orderly pattern, a natural progression from one theme to another as ideas were developed, debated, matured, and incorporated into different approaches.

Whether we have succeeded will rest with those who read this text. It has, for us, been a learning experience as we have searched for source material, "got to know" different authors and approaches, and tried to understand the different influences of the time. We may well, at times, have been influenced by those we quote and refer to as we read and thought about their views on stress. In the end though, there is, running through this volume, and those of other author's, a remarkable consistency that reflects the passion with which points of view are argued and the desire that writers have to provide insights into what is going on. It is to all those who have contributed to the field that we are indebted.

A book like this could not be written without help. While we take responsibility for the views and ideas expressed we would like to thank a number of people who gave us access to their copies of original material. Our thanks go to Dr Rob Briner, Department of Organizational Psychology at Birkbeck College, Professor Tom Cox, CBE, Institute of Work – Health and Organizations, University of Nottingham, Professor David Guest at Kings College, University of London, and Professor Roger Williams, Erasmus University, Rotterdam. Our thanks and acknowledgment also goes to Associate Professor Clemens Weikert and Professor Sten-Olaf Brenner at the Centre for Work, Health, and Organizational Learning at Kristianstad University who provided us with the material on the history of stress in Sweden.

Cary Cooper CBE   Philip Dewe
Lancaster   London

CHAPTER ONE

From Early Beginnings to the Twentieth Century

Introduction

The fact that the concept of stress has, over the past six decades, been "the source of immense interest" (Doublet, 2000, p.41) should not disguise the fact that the term has steadily evolved over a period of several hundred years, if not over centuries, and "its discovery in the twentieth century was more of a rediscovery" (Cassidy, 1999, p.6). In order to explain its origins and meanings, authors have taken a number of different strategies. Some point to the possibility that the word "stress" may have been derived from the Latin *stringere* (to draw tight) and go on to explore how, over the centuries, a "large number of variant words can be found in the English literature" (Cox, 1978, p.2). Some focus on the scientific use and investigation of the term and trace this meaning back around 50 years (Jex, 1998). While others begin by tracing the scientific origins of the term "stress" to its first appearance in *Psychological Abstracts* in 1944 (Jones and Bright, 2001), or simply make the point, that while it may be difficult to accept, before the 1940s, the term was "almost unknown outside of the engineering profession" (Haward, 1960, p.185). All have unwittingly being drawn into the debate concerning not just when the term "stress" was popularized, but who was the first to popularize it (see Appley and Trumbull, 1967; Bartlett, 1998; Mason, 1975a).

Some authors, considering the evolution of the term "stress," describe how, from the idea of hardship in the seventeenth century, it's meaning evolved through the eighteenth and nineteenth centuries to reflect some sort of force, pressure, or strain, and how this latter sense of the word was "taken over into science" and probably helped to reinforce its popular usage (Hinkle, 1973, p.32). However, the view that the present use of the term has "only recently emerged" as a result of it being taken over by scientists and social scientists, is a somewhat tentative conclusion to draw (Newton, 1995, p.50) – as Bartlett (1998) shows the idea that "stress" can influence health has a long history. This means that there can be "no simple privileged position of social scientists in inventing our contemporary under-standing of stress" (Newton, 1995, p.50). If this is the case, then an examination of the historical origins of the word will allow us to consider whether stress is a disease of our times; whether, over the years, there has been any consistency in the use of the term; whether in some guise or another it has always been with us – hence its long history; whether whatever the "label used they have all attempted to explain some aspects of the relationship that people have with their environment" (Doublet, 2000, p.78); and whether by exploring these issues we get some insight into the social purposes the term has served (Pollock, 1988).

We begin our inquiry into the historical origins of the concept of "stress" by setting out two themes, which are not mutually exclusive, that have influenced the meaning and use of the term. The first theme is that over the centuries "various nonphysical phenomena have been advanced as either possible causes of diseases or factors contributing to diseases" (Doublet, 2000, p.41). So, at various times in history "conditions" like hysteria, passions, vapors, nerves, neurasthenia, worry, mental strain, and tension have been put forward as significant contributors of or explanations for disease (see Doublet, 2000, pp.41–79). The second theme is that these conditions carry with them the notion that "life places difficult demands on individuals, who then succumb under the strain to psychological or biological disease" (Abbott, 2001, p.37). The idea that the stresses and strains of modern life – the individuals' ability to cope with the pace of life – became an almost ritualistic belief in the nineteenth century (Abbott, 2001), and in the twentieth century the pace of life was viewed as the root cause of much illness and disease. These two themes suggest that for centuries alongside "bio-logical medicine there has always been some kind of additional explanation of disease" (Doublet, 2000, p.77), centered around different sorts of "conditions" such as those identified above; and that despite the fact that many of these earlier "conditions" or explanations were not entirely based on any empirical evidence, their significance lay in the way they attempted to explain illness in terms of the relationship between the person and the environment.

Hooke's Law and the Engineering Analogy

A number of authors (Hinkle, 1973; Newton, 1995) indicate that there has been a fair degree of consistency in the use of the term "stress" from at least the seventeenth century onwards. "Stress" in the seventeenth century had come to mean "hardship" (Hinkle, 1973). It was towards the end of this century that the word assumed a more technical importance (Lazarus, 1993) through the writing of Robert Hooke, whose work was to result in an engineering analogy of stress. Hooke's work was concerned with how man-made structures (e.g. bridges) could be made to withstand heavy loads without collapsing (Engel, 1985; Hinkle, 1973; Lazarus, 1999). What Hooke gave us through his *Law of Elasticity* was "load," the demand placed on the structure, "stress" that area affected by the demand, and "strain" the change in form that results from the interaction between load and stress (Cox, 1978; Engel, 1985; Lazarus, 1993; 1999). Despite the difficulties involved in the transition from physics to other disciplines, the similarities of these terms with contemporary terms are startling, and reflects the influence of Hooke's work and its survival into modern times via the idea that stress is an external demand placed on a bio-social-psychological system (Lazarus, 1993).

Hooke's work represents an important episode in the history of stress (Doublet, 2000). The engineering analogy and the idea of the body as machine-like, proved to be fertile ground for two other ideas that have profoundly influenced thinking about stress. The first idea follows from the reasoning that "if the body were like a machine and machines are subject to wear and tear then so too would be the body" (Doublet, 2000, p.48). So, into the discourse on stress, came the idea of the impact on the body of the wear and tear of life (see Doublet, 2000; Selye, 1956). The second idea to emerge was that, like a machine, the body needs some energy to help it function. Depending on the amount of this energy, the body will, like a machine, perform well, poorly, or even stop (Doublet, 2000). This energy was assumed to be a product of the nervous system, and scientists very quickly began to speak in terms of the "depletion of nervous energy" and "disorders of the nerves" (Doublet, 2000, p.49).

The seventeenth century and the writings of Descartes also left an indelible mark, if not on the concept of "stress" itself, then at least on the emerging field of psychology, the discipline of many contemporary stress researchers. Descartes' work confronted an age-old problem, the relationship between the mind and the body, by suggesting, "that the non-physical mind could influence the physical body" (Hergenhahn, 1992, p.98). Throughout the centuries, almost every conceivable position that can be taken has been taken in trying to explain the nature of the relationship between the mind and the body (Hergenhahn, 1992), and more particularly, how to resolve the impasse "stemming from the difficulty in explaining how the non-physical mind interacts with the physical world. This physical world necessarily includes our brain and body" (Doublet, 2000 p.48). At present the mind–body problem may not be resolvable (Valentine, 1982). Perhaps we can do no better in this debate than to adopt Descartes' common-sense approach to the mind–body relationship: "Everyone, he said, has both bodily and conscious experiences and senses the fact that the two influence one another" (Hergenhahn, 1992, p.99).

The Eighteenth Century and Beyond

The eighteenth century, as Doublet points out, saw a return of what he calls the "passions," e.g. nerves, vapors, hysteria, as explanations for different illnesses and disease. The use of such conditions as tools for explaining different complaints led writers of the time to conclude that "at least a third of all diseases were of nervous origin" (Doublet, 2000, p.49). Scientists and social commentators of the time also continued to point to the quickening pace of life and the impact this was having on health and well-being, to the extent that by the time the nineteenth century arrived, there was clearly a fear that "the human nervous system was ill-adapted to cope with the increased complexity of modern life" (see Wozniak, 1992, p.4). Wozniak further illustrates the nature of this fear by referring to the work of George Beard

(1839–83), a noted American physician specializing in diseases of the nervous system. Beard's work led him to suggest that pressing demands of nineteenth-century life may lead to a circuit overload of the nervous system. Beard described this state as "neurasthenia" – "a weakness of the nervous system" (Rosenberg, 1962, p.240); "nervous exhaustion" characterized by symptoms such as morbid anxiety, unaccountable fatigue, and irrational fears caused by the inability of the nervous system to meet the demands of daily life. The idea that the "stresses and strains of modern life could cause mental disease was 'an almost ritualistic belief' of the nineteenth century" (Abbott, 2001, p.37), and the diagnosis of nervous exhaustion became "part of the office furniture of most physicians" (Rosenberg, 1962, p.258). During its heyday "which lasted from the 1870s to the turn of the century, the diagnosis of neurasthenia provided patients with a scientifically legitimate explanation of their inability to perform their expected roles" (Martensen, 1994, p.1243).

Beard's work was important for two reasons. The first because he helped to "remove the social disapproval attached to such ailments" and "helped make their diagnosis a medical and not a moral one" (Rosenberg, 1962, p.253). Secondly, and more importantly, his work deserves serious consideration because it was an "attempt to shed light upon the role played by society in the production of mental illness" (Rosenberg, 1962, p.253), and it is this aspect that makes his work relevant today. To Beard, nervous exhaustion was an immediate consequence of "a particular kind of social organization; it was as peculiar a product of the nineteenth century as the telegraph" (Rosenberg, 1962, p.253). Even though by the early twentieth century, neurasthenia had "lost most of its validity as a diagnosis" (Martensen, 1994, p.1243), it can be viewed as "one of the growing pains of a new and better society" (Rosenberg, 1962, p.257).

It was also during this time (1859) that Claude Bernard, a noted French physician, first introduced the idea that the internal environment of living organisms must remain fairly constant in response to changes in the external environment (Cassidy, 1999; Monat and Lazarus, 1991; Selye, 1983). For Bernard, the most striking feature of living organisms was their harmonious arrangements. The idea of harmony and consistency within living organisms gave rise to his notion of the internal environment or the *milieu intérieur*. Bernard pointed out that that it is the fixity of the *milieu intérieur* that is the condition of free and independent life (see Selye, 1983). The fixity of the *milieu intérieur* refers to the idea that nothing within the body must be allowed to deviate far from what is normal; if something does, then the individual will become ill or may even die (see Selye, 1973). Survival, according to Bernard is determined by consistent maintenance of the internal environment via "continual compensatory reactions" (Doublet, 2000, p.55) in response to changes in the external environment. The significance of Bernard's work lies in the necessary receptive atmosphere it created for the eventual development of the contemporary notion of stress. His more lasting legacy was the motivation his work gave to later researchers to take forward his pioneering studies and explore the nature of those adaptive changes by which the steady state is maintained (Selye, 1991).

Bernard's work reflected the mechanistic view of biology (Mason, 1972). According to this view, there was nothing mysterious about life simply because "the behavior of all organisms, including humans, can be explained in the same way that the behavior of any machine can be explained – that is in terms of its parts and the laws governing those parts" (Hergenhahn, 1992, p.17). Bernard's work may have been a response to those who adopted a "vitalist" point of view (Cassidy, 1999). The vitalists "maintained that life could not be explained by the interactions of physical and chemical processes alone" (Hergenhahn, 1992, p.213). To the vitalists, life was something more. Humans possessed some "vital force" or "life force," and so could never be understood simply in terms of mechanical laws. About the time that Bernard's work was being debated, Charles Darwin's writings were about to deromanticize nature and give to the world a mechanistic view of evolution (see Leahey, 1992), providing another impetus to the mechanistic view of biology and science and the mechanization of human nature. So, by the end of the nineteenth century, it is probably useful to note that one conflict underlies all others: the conflict between the beliefs of scientific mechanism which reduce the individual "to a collection of chemicals laboring in a vast industrial machine" (Leahey, 1992, p.171) on the one hand, and the "spiritual reality" of the individual on the other.

Bernard's work, like other scientists of his time, adopted a "reductionist perspective" (Cassidy, 1999). Reductionism is where the ideas of one field (in this case human behavior) are explained in terms of the terminology and laws of another field (in this case biology-physiology). In this sense, the phenomena of one field are "being reduced" to the principles of another (see Hergenhahn, 1992; Leahey, 1992). Adopting a reductionist approach at this time is not surprising, since the prevailing disease model of illness "held that illness results from external agents that disrupt the body's normal function" (Aldwin, 2000, p.2) and that health could only be regained by restoring the body to normal functioning. Viewed in this way, the prevailing assumptions about causality would naturally lead researchers to the physiological constitution of the body. Much had and has been learned from this approach. The need to explain disease through an "exact science" therefore dominated, and the idea that the mind, mental processes, or some "vital force" animated physiological functioning ran counter to the accepted mechanistic views and fell "largely on deaf ears" (Wittkower, 1977, p.4). Against this ideal, that only the objective mechanistic methods of science could yield knowledge, the views of the vitalists could not prevail but neither were they "conquered" (Leahey, 1992, p.172). The end of the nineteenth century was to see the emergence of the three founding forms (consciousness, unconscious, and adaptation) of psychology: "All the concepts for each were in place, awaiting only the creative minds and forceful personalities needed to weld them into coherent psychological programs" (Leahey, 1992, p.172).

Summary: Themes from the Eighteenth and Nineteenth Centuries

As the nineteenth century drew to a close, a number of threads – some centuries old – were beginning to form into patterns that would provide the underlay for the rich tapestry of developments in the twentieth century. A number of these are worth emphasizing again. Perhaps the most significant is that over the centuries various nonphysical "conditions" have been put forward to explain illness and disease which "all seem to have attempted to explain some aspect of the relationship that people have with their environment" (Doublet, 2000, p.78). While at times the significance of these "conditions" has been sidelined, as have the methods to investigate them by the power of the scientific paradigm, they nevertheless have resulted in a discourse that bears a startling resemblance to the familiar discourse of the twentieth century. Three of these themes – the idea of "wear and tear," the concept of the "steady state," and the impact of the "pace of life" are as robustly discussed today in relation to the nature of "stress," as they had been in the preceding centuries. Whether these themes are anymore powerful in the context of twentieth-century discoveries is yet to be explored.

Two other themes appeared to hint at what was yet to come. The first theme concerns the dominance of the "scientific" approach and the belief that "because it was non-physical, the 'life force' was forever beyond the scope of scientific analysis" (Hergenhahn, 1992. p.212). Anyone suspected of being a vitalist was therefore regarded as "unscientific" (Hergenhahn, 1992). So, as the twentieth century drew near, the pursuit of knowledge that searches for general laws of functioning (nomothetic), was regarded as the only one capable of providing a "scientific" approach, leaving the idiographic mode ("that entails the pursuit of personalized qualities and individual uniqueness") unable to demonstrate its rich explanatory power (Blundell, 1975, p.17). The irony is that a scientific movement which owes so much to Darwin neglected the "Darwinian emphasis on subtle variations between individuals" (Blundell, 1975, p.18). Finally, there is the second theme or question of whether the different "conditions" or "labels" used to explain illness served a social purpose? That purpose was, as Pollock suggests, "to reduce the arbitrariness of suffering" (1988, p.390), and to provide a legitimate explanation for why individuals were unable to perform their roles or deal with the pace of life. Neurasthenia, for example, "helped make sense of symptoms that otherwise would have been found reprehensible, such as an inability to function in the home or office" (Martensen, 1994, p.1243). If neurasthenia was one of those wonderful nineteenth-century diagnostic entities "that promised something for almost everyone involved" (Martensen, 1994, p.1243), was this just a taste, a hint, of things to come?

CHAPTER TWO

The Twentieth Century: The Early Years

Introduction

The twentieth century was to be "the century of science and technology, with the excitement of new discoveries tempered by the ever increasing pace of life" (Doublet, 2000, p.65). The early years of the century saw a number of developments that would draw researchers even closer to what is now simply taken for granted – that the phenomenon they were studying could be described as "stress." These developments included the increasing use of the term "stress" in discourse about human existence, the emergence in the field of psychology of the notion of *functionalism*, the early concerns about *work performance*, the preoccupation with *fatigue and mental hygiene* and the first tentative steps towards, and the growing acceptance of, psychosocial explanations of illness. To say that the word "stress" had by the early twentieth century "come to be used as an analogue in the social and biological sciences to describe a possible cause of ill health and mental disease" (Bartlett, 1998, p.24) needs a little explaining. Its use was frequently coupled with "strain," with "stress" resulting in "strain," a reflection of its engineering roots. It was also closely associated with ideas of "hardship" and different adverse circumstances. Doublet (2000, pp.65–8) points to the use of the term "mechanical stress" in the early part of the twentieth century to account for structural damage of the body, and the use by doctors of the terms "stress, strain, and worry" to explain the medical effects of the pressures of early-twentieth-century life. The links between "hard work and worry" and "stress and strain" soon became commonly discussed in the early years of that century (Hinkle, 1987). Whatever the term and whatever its

meaning, the search by early-twentieth-century scientists reflected just another attempt in a long tradition of attempts trying
to explain the individuals relationship with the environment.
Other developments were taking place that would draw researchers closer to a concept of "stress."

The Emergence of the School of Functionalism

It was also around this time – the beginning of the twentieth
century – that the methodologies, conceptual and substantive
boundaries of psychology were greatly expanded by the emergence of the school of "functionalism." Functionalism is described as "a general and broadly presented point of view that
stresses the analysis of mind and behavior in terms of their
function rather than in terms of their contents" (Reber, 1985,
p.290). Despite this description, functionalism, it is generally
agreed, is difficult to define, but it directed attention to the
"how" questions, and was concerned with the "function of
mental and behavioral processes" (Hergenhahn, 1992, p.329).
Keenly interested in being "socially useful"(Leahey, 1992,
p.289), its aim was to explore a "host of interesting problems
that affected the daily lives of people" (Viney, 1993, p.284),
including those of emotional disorders and the work environment. Furthermore, it "refused to be restricted by narrow con-
ceptions of the scientific method" (Viney, 1993, p.284). What they
rejected was a psychology that was almost entirely focused on
basic science. The functionalists were to emphasize the discovery
of facts (basic science), but the distinctiveness of their approach
lay in trying to understand what difference the facts made
(applied science). Functionalism was fueled by the pragmatism
and progressivism of early-twentieth-century America, where
"reform, efficiency and progress" (Leahey, 1992, p.00) became
the activating values. Functionalism was based around the idea
that psychology should be practical and should make a difference. Its interest was towards "what consciousness does" and
how it aids individuals in adapting to a changing environment. It
was a psychology of mental adjustment.

It was the American, William James (1842–1910), who is
credited with laying the foundations for what was to become
the "school of functionalism." Yet it appears that functionalism

soon lost its distinctiveness as a school of thought because "most of its major tenets were assimilated into all forms of psychology" (Hergenhahn, 1992, p.331). Despite functionalism being criticized as being "too vague" and "too eclectic" (Viney, 1993, pp.284-5), a number of common themes can be identified that express its main tenets. A number of these help to explain the "virtual explosion of interest in applied psychology" (Viney, 1993, p.285) and help to describe the world of contemporary psychology. These themes (see Hergenhahn, 1992, pp.300-1) included, for example, the desire to understand the function of the mind in relation to individual adaptation, to apply research findings to the improvement of personal life, to urge a broadening of methods in pursuit of these goals, and to provide a psychology that makes a difference to life. This climate of pragmatism and wanting to make a difference, provided a fertile ground for early concerns about work performance and the preoccupation with fatigue and mental hygiene.

Fatigue and Mental Hygiene

As researchers moved into the twentieth century, two literatures central to the development of the stress concept – fatigue and mental hygiene – were taken as "signs of the individual's failure to successfully *adjust* to modern life" (Abbott, 2001, p.41). The "closest to stress theorizing that one can come" at the beginning of this century, suggests Newton, were the fatigue studies (1995, p.23); sentiments echoed by Hearnshaw who argued that fatigue studies were the earliest precursors of current stress discourse (1987). The work on fatigue was grounded in scientific management's concern for work performance and provided a "psychological answer" to what was perceived as the problems of industrial efficiency (Newton, 1995). The onset of the First World War and the issues surrounding wartime production also made researchers minds receptive to the problems of fatigue. Early writers clearly saw the link between fatigue and performance, and wrote about "the influence of fatigue on industrial achievement" (Munsterberg, 1913, p.211) and "fatigue effects not only the adjustment of the individual but influences very directly the welfare of society at large" (Viteles, 1932, p.440), to the extent that there should be "as little waste as possible, whether of individual effort or of capital" (Muscio, 1974, p.25).

Fatigue was regarded as both a mental and physiological phe-nomenon, with its mental dimension being described "as the feeling of tiredness or weariness" (Muscio, 1974, p.47) or nervous fatigue or "brain fag" resulting from the production of muscular energy (Viteles, 1932). By the 1920s, fatigue had become a meta-phor for that "tired, run-down feeling," with popular magazines debating "the real meaning of fatigue" (Abbott, 2001, p.41). Nevertheless, these authors delivered a psychology that was finely tuned to the daily lives of people and presented a broader vision of what psychology should be. The key to their work lay in the argument made by Munsterberg that psychologists should "acquaint themselves with the world of work" and "then struc-ture research on the basis of real issues encountered in daily life" (Viney, 1993, pp.267–8).

The problems of "mental hygiene" were also grounded in work performance and industrial efficiency. Here the emphasis was on the "diagnosis and treatment of the minor mental troubles of the manager or the worker before they produced major and disabling problems" (Rose, 1999, p.69). At the heart of this approach was the "notion of the 'efficient use' of the individual in society, the idea of adjustment through [mental] hygiene" (Abbott, 2001, p.42). Two themes captured the spirit of the mental hygiene movement. The first was the organization of the workplace so as to "minimize the production of symptoms of emotional and mental stability and enhance adjustment" (Rose, 1999, p.69). The second, in a not dissimilar vein, was concerned with the maladjusted worker, where minor mental disturbances in the worker represented a loss in industrial effi-ciency which could only be regained by the worker achieving maximal mental health. The focus on the mental health of the worker was soon to lead to the development of ergonomics, where the physical and mental capacities of the worker were fused with the design of equipment to "produce an optimal productive and efficient labour process" (Rose, 1999, p.89). It also led to the development of the psychoanalysis of the organ-ization, to be made famous by the Tavistock Institute of Human Relations (Rose, 1999). The focus on fatigue and mental hygiene spurred on by the desire for industrial efficiency, reinforced by the needs of war, and captured by the enthusiasm for the principles of functionalism, provided the active ingredients to produce the new and clearly demarcated field of industrial psychology. But there was also a real sense that industrial efficiency could be achieved "without the sacrifice of individual welfare" (Viteles, 1932, p.18), hence the marrying of what Newton (1995, p.52) describes as the "humanistic and the economic," helping to differentiate this new field of applied psychology from the rigors of scientific management.

Psychosomatic Medicine and the Contribution of Walter Cannon

The early decades of the twentieth century also saw more attention being given to an idea that had for centuries been recognized by "progressive physicians," that of the role of the mind in physical illness and the notion of "internal conflict" as a basis of mental disease (Wittkower, 1977). These ideas were to find more formal expression through the rise of *psychosomatic medicine*. This movement grew out of a reaction to the machine age of medicine, where studying a person simply as a biological organism could no longer sustain a model of illness, and slowly the idea that "disease may be as much a result of the adaptive reactions of the host as they are of the damaging effects of pathogenic agents" (Hinkle, 1977, p.28) gained ground. The human element was being reintroduced to medicine. The idea that the "relation of people to the other people around them and to the society in which they live are important causes of disease" (Hinkle, 1977, p.28) began to gain acceptance along with the idea that thoughts, motives and feelings had to be taken into account in understanding disease. These views along with their historical antecedents were "a reaction against the reductionist view, carried over from nineteenth-century medicine, of health and disease as states that could be explained adequately without any reference to those attributes that made man [*sic*] human. Thus psychosomatic medicine developed as a *reformist movement*" (Lipowski, 1977, p.xiv).

Psychosomatic medicine, since its beginnings in the 1920s, has followed two major directions (see Lipowski, 1977 p.xiii). The first took inspiration from psychoanalytic theory and emphasized the importance of unconscious conflicts and the use of effective therapies to resolve such conflicts. The second focused on conscious and measurable psychological variables such as emotions seeking to understand the association between them and, for example the incidence, timing, and the degree of severity of illness. Both these directions had one common goal: "to establish the precise role of man's [sic] symbolic processes and their emotional correlates in modifying bodily functions and especially in contributing to the development, course, and outcome of human disease" (Lipowski, 1977, p.xiv). Quite simply, psychosomatic medicine was interested in the relationship between emotions and disease.

The Work of Walter Cannon

One scientist who paved the way for the introduction of the psychosomatic approach is Walter Cannon. Cannon's work (see for example, 1914, 1920, 1928, 1935, and 1939) spanned three decades. He was a "great inspiration" (Selye, 1975, p.39) for those whose work was to follow. Contemporary writers on stress still draw on his images of homeostasis and fight or flight reactions. His legacy rests on the fact that his work is still often used as the starting point of how stress occurs, and so it is worth paying some attention to his different ideas. Cannon's philosophy is in many ways captured by the way he explains the title of his book *The Wisdom of the Body*. Inspired by an address given by Professor Starling of University College, London, in 1923 he was greatly taken by Starling's declaration that "only by understanding the wisdom of the body, shall we attain that mastery of disease and pain which will enable us to relieve the burden of mankind" (1939, p.xv). Because Cannon's views "coincided with those of Professor Starling and because the facts and interpretations Cannon offered illustrated Starling's point of view, Cannon chose to give the title of Starling's oration to the present volume" (1939, p.xv).

Cannon first gave us the concept of "homeostasis." In the main, this idea pertains to "the relation of the autonomic system to the self-regulation of physiological processes" (Cannon, 1939, pp.xiii–xiv). Homeostasis – "staying power" (Selye, 1982) – or the body's ability to maintain its own consistency had long impressed biologists. Cannon, for example, refers to the work of the Belgian physiologist Leon Fredericq, who in 1885, declared "the living being is an agency of such sort that each disturbing influence induces by itself the calling forth of compensatory activity to neutralize or repair the disturbance" (1939, p.21). Cannon described this self-regulation in terms of the basis of our existence in the face of fundamentally disturbing conditions is dependent on the presence and stability of a "fluid matrix" in which our body parts exist. He went on to add that the physiological activities, which maintain the steady states in the individual, are so complex that there should be a "special designation" for them one that he went on to call "homeostasis." The word, Cannon maintained, was not meant to imply something static. It meant a condition – a condition that may alter but which is relatively stable. Cannon's thesis was that if threatened by change then that change was immediately signaled and corrective mechanisms swung into action to avert the threat or restore the normal. If we are to be effective, Cannon argued, the individual environment, which is part of us, must remain relatively stable. For this internal environment to be consistently maintained, every change and every reaction in relation to the external environment must be accompanied by a compensatory process in the inner environment of the person. This rectifying process operates through the sympathetic division of the autonomic system.

The importance of Cannon's work on homeostasis rests as much in the way that it echoed concerns from the past, as it did in providing a pathway for the future. Cannon (1935) was interested in what he described as the "efficiency" of the regulatory mechanisms to maintain stability. If it was possible to understand the force and endurance of these regulatory processes, he went on to argue, it might then be possible to identify the limits beyond which stress overpowers these corrective mechanisms and fundamentally changes the steady state. Is there, he asks (making use of an engineering analogy), a "safety factor" that allows for these contingencies. Staying with this engineering theme and the way our bodies are built, Cannon marveled at the way in which, over many decades, our bodily systems whilst, being continually battered by the wear and tear of life, are at the same time being continuously restored through a process of repair (Cannon, 1939). Alternatively, he suggested, maybe individuals have by one means or another learnt ways to maintain stability and uniformity, and are capable of keeping a steady state even in the face of events which generally would be expected to be deeply troubling. Maintaining this evolutionary theme, is there, Cannon pondered, some way where by these regulatory processes increasingly become, over time, more efficient (Cannon, 1935).

Cannon also talked about the "vitality" of the individual as expressed in the individuals considered ability to respond without disturbing the stability of the internal environment (Cannon, 1935), reflecting themes of adaptation and individual differences. Cannon (1939) also pointed to what could be described as a development theme associated with homeostasis. He called attention to the fact that for as long as our internal environment is kept stable, then individuals are free from the constraints of demanding forces that could be distressing. When the question of "freedom for what?" was raised, Cannon responded by suggesting that it was freedom for higher-level activity of the nervous system "to fully develop and amply express our imagination, insight, and skill" (Canon, 1939, pp.302–3). So Cannon argued, if it was possible to establish a method of "assaying the efficiency" of the bodies regulatory processes, then we would have a framework for determining how different sorts of human experience affect the mechanisms which determine homeostasis (Cannon, 1935).

Cannon was also interested in instincts (Newton, 1995), and in the bodily changes that took place in "great emotional excitement" (Cannon, 1939). The most widely applicable explanation Cannon argued, for these natural responses, is that over a long period of evolutionary experience they have become developed for rapid service in the battle for survival (Cannon, 1920). There is, he added, an established association between particular emotions and peculiar instinctive reactions. Fear and anger, argued Cannon (1939), have served as a preparation for action. "Fear has become associated with the instinct to run, to escape; and anger or aggressive feeling, with the instinct to attack. These are fundamental emotions and instincts" that have developed over generations as individuals engaged in the struggle for existence (Cannon, 1939, p.227). This reaction was labeled the "fight or flight" response. This fight or flight notion would ultimately come to play an important role in stress discourse (Doublet, 2000). In response to a threat or "stress," the fight or flight response made it possible for a person to "more effectively meet the challenges, through mobilizing mental and physical abilities" (Aldwin, 2000, p, 27).

This response was perceived by Cannon (1914) to be a general response to any "stress" – physical or social. He believed "that the body responds to all threats in a similar manner, *whether-or-not that manner is immediately relevant*" (Aldwin, 2000, p.28). Cannon (1914, p.278) expressed the general nature of the flight or fight response in this way. The emotions of fear and rage, he argued, accompany the body's preparation for action and though the events, which provoke them, are likely to result in fight or flight in either case the body's needs are essentially the same.

One of the interesting issues surrounding Cannon's work is the question concerning "what was he referring to when he talked about stress?" The fact that Cannon is, in some histories of stress, regarded as a "founding father" seems in "many ways a strange choice" as "he hardly refers to stress at all" (Newton, 1995, p.19). It is true that he does at different times refer to the "stress" placed upon an agent (Cannon, 1935, p.7) or "great emotional stress" (Cannon, 1914, p.261). However, it is probable that the term was being used in a physiological sense (Mason, 1975a), where the "stress" more often than not referred to heat, hunger, cold, or loss of oxygen. Cannon, according to Hinkle (1973), more likely used the term in a quasi-scientific sense, prompted by the need to express the environment within which the mechanisms of homeostasis operated. His approach was clearly biological and evolutionary biology at that (Cassidy, 1999). It is possible (see Mason, 1975a) to get an insight into Cannon's views on "emotional stress" by considering his 1928 paper on "The mechanism of emotional disturbance of bodily functions."

Cannon makes it clear at the outset of this paper that the indifference shown by doctors and their failure to take seriously the emotional elements of disease stems from the powerful scientific methodologies of the day, where "any state which has no distinct 'pathology' appears to be unreal or of minor significance" (1928, p.877). Because, he goes on, fears and worries have no clear pathway then they were not seen as troubles with which doctors should concern themselves. Faced with this indifference by doctors it is no wonder, Cannon argued, that patients turned to others who were accepting of the legitimacy of these troubling states. As a physiologist, Cannon believed that he had a reasonable right to consider those physiological processes which accompany "profound emotional experience." But the importance of exploring emotional experiences was because they were seen as being "causally related" to, or possibly accompanied by, a "demonstrable lesion," and it was only when one was seen as accompanying the other that they were explored and effectively treated (1928, p.877). Yet despite the fact that Canon discussed emotions throughout in physiological terms, from the point of view of having a "typical reaction pattern," the significance he gave to exploring the concept of "emotional stress" is best expressed in the conclusions to his 1928 paper. Cannon argued, that if the doctor is concerned with the way the body works and those factors which trouble it, then the doctor should equally be concerned with the impact of "emotion stress" and how it should be tackled. This field, Cannon argued, "has not been well cultivated. Much work still needs to be done in it. It offers to all kinds of medical practitioners many opportunities for useful studies. There is no more fascinating realm of medicine in which to conduct investigation. I heartily commend it to you" (1928, p.884).

Cannon was also interested in what he described as the "relations of biological and social homeostasis." He was interested in whether or not general principles of stabilization applied across society and wondered whether it might be instructive to explore other organizational structures – industrial, domestic, or social – in the light of the way the body mobilizes against threat (Cannon, 1939). To Cannon the feature of society that most closely corresponded to the "fluid matrix" could be found in the different aspects of the distribution system. The stability of this system would be met by the "certainty of continuous delivery" and the "continuous remuneration of labour" not "in a fixed and rigid social system but in such adaptable industrial and commercial functions as assure continuous supplies of elementary human needs" (1939, p.315). It is here that Cannon again turns to the idea of individual development and growth. He suggests that it is of considerable significance that people's suffering as a result of instability in the social system has resulted in increased attention being directed towards improvement. Cannon concludes that the main service of social homeostasis would be to support bodily homeostasis: "It would therefore help to release the highest activities of the nervous system for adventure and achievement. With essential needs assured, the priceless unessentials could be freely sought" (1939, p.323).

Cannon's work clearly reflects the social reformist ideals of the psychosomatic movement. The concept of "homeostasis, like that of a *'milieu intérieur'*, its predecessor 70 years earlier, would make the notion of stress possible" (Doublet, 2000, p.71). Without homeostasis argues Doublet "the concept of 'stress' would not be necessary" (2000, p.71). His explanation of homeostasis, coupled with the fight or flight response, where the internal environment is preserved by the production of compensatory adjustments, became, for many researchers who followed, the starting point for how stress occurs. His work, however, is not without its critics. Critiques of his work fall into three categories. The first relates to the *nature of the concept of homeostasis* itself, and are less in the way of criticisms and more in the way of points of clarification. First, there is the need to clarify whether there is ever a state where all problems are solved. Homeostasis, it is postulated, is "merely a state toward which the organism may tend, but which is never fully attained" (Howard and Scott, 1965, p.145). Secondly, there is the idea that *homeostasis is best understood in relative terms*, that is, "equilibrium in any given environment field can be appreciated only if we view it with respect to equilibrium in other environmental fields" (Howard and Scott, 1965, p.145). Is, for example, equilibrium in one field maintained at the expense of equilibrium in another? Finally there is the issue of whether, when considering the concept of homeostasis, some account needs to be taken of those *individuals who introduce disequilibrium* simply to test their problem-solving ability, particularly in those environments where there is a sense of resolution (Howard and Scott, 1965).

A second category of comment reflects on Cannon's views of "our biologic nature" and its "constant struggle with society" (Newton, 1995, p.22). Newton (1995) draws attention to two issues regarding the biological nature of stress. The first is that "it places responsibility for stress on our (biological) selves;" and secondly it "tells us that there is nothing we can do about it" (1995, p.23) except perhaps to modify our instincts. This latter point refers to the notion that has grown up around the flight or fight response. What was once an appropriate instinctive response is now no longer appropriate to the modern age; an idea prompted by Cannon's view on the appropriate satisfaction of instincts and "whilst we have developed technologically and socially" our nature has not "evolved sufficiently" to deal with the problems of contemporary society (Newton, 1995, p.22). The idea, as Newton makes clear, that individuals "must buckle down and address the problems in themselves and their unfortunate inheritance of outworn instincts" (1995, p.23) has quickly found its way into popular stress discourse.

Finally, there is the issue caught up in Cannon's idea regarding the "wisdom of the body," as to whether the body's "self-regulation entailed a form of wisdom or self knowledge" (Sullivan, 1990, p.493) such that "the body is an agent of its own health" (Doublet, 2000, p.152) with some form of "self knowing and self healing powers" (Sullivan, 1990, p.494). This, however, would seem to run counter to Cannon's view that the body responds instinctively, and it is doubtful that such instinctive responses "could be construed to be indicative of knowledge or wisdom. Furthermore, the proposition that the body can 'monitor' its own state at a subconscious level is questionable" (Doublet, 2000, p.153). While the work of Cannon will continue to be debated, all theories of stress that were to follow his work rely, either implicitly or explicitly, on some form of homeostasis or compensatory activity. This reflects both the power of his ideas, and the coherence they lent to a rapidly expanding field.

Hans Selye

Selye's contribution to the field of stress is without doubt one of great importance (Mason, 1975a). His research had an extraordinary impact on biology and medicine, and his work created an "aura of academic excitement and controversy" (Mason, 1971, p.323). Described as a "celebrant of stress" (Newton, 1995, p.19), there is, Lazarus (1977) comments, possibly no person in recent times who has influenced stress theory and research more than Hans Selye. But can he be credited with discovering "stress?" Perhaps the simplest way to enter into the spirit of this concept, argued Selye, would be to explore its historical roots. But then he added, there is the difficulty of where to start. The natural place to start, he went on, would be with the discovery of stress but it seemed to Selye, that even this is not so straight forward, because in a way the condition of stress has always been with us even if the significance of the concept was not recognized. "Perhaps this is true of every fundamental concept; it is not easy to recognize discovery" (Selye, 1956, p.5).

Selye then goes on to argue that discovery is always a matter of viewpoint and degree. "Whenever we single out an individual as *the* discoverer of anything, we merely mean that for us he [*sic*] discovered it more than anyone else" (1956, p.5). To this, Selye adds that discovery is *"not to* see *something first, but to establish solid connections between the previously known and the hitherto unknown that constitutes the essence of scientific discovery"* (1956, p.6). If so, then Selye would certainly accept that his work brought together different parts of the "stress" concept into a workable theory. To him this constituted the very nature of discovery. *"To discover does not mean to* see, *but to uncover sufficiently that many can* see *and continue to* see *forever"* (1956, p.38). The last word must be left to Selye. He was quite emphatic. What he discovered (Selye, 1975), he made quite clear, was the *stress syndrome* and certainly not stress. For Selye, his contribution stemmed from the fact that he demonstrated that there was such a phenomenon as a non-specific response pattern. It was this, he argued, that represented his initial contribution.

The Concept of Non-specificity

Selye was motivated to accomplish something meaningful. To him meaningfulness required him to "muster the self-discipline and enforce the scientific exactness which is so necessary to do anything in my field" (1979, p.21). "In my life," he noted in his autobiography, "I shall have accomplished only one thing: a better understanding of stress" (1979, p.22). Selye's goal was to devote his working life to providing a theory of stress ("his cathedral") that would reach a significant level of maturity that would ensure its survival and development. Selye's journey was not without controversy, and doubts still remain as to the "maturity" of his theory. However, there is no mistaking the durability of the concept, if not Selye's ideas, and this "suggests that a continuing search for what is solid and valid in these [stress] concepts may eventually prove rewarding" (Mason, 1975a, p.6). Selye's work can be divided into two parts: before and after the Second World War. His work before the war explains the way it all started, whilst his work following the war, describes the development and subsequent debate surrounding his "adaptation syndrome."

In 1926, as a second year medical student, Selye first came across what he noted as some type of stereotypical response of the body to any demand made upon it. Why, Selye questioned, did patients suffering from a whole range of diseases all seem to have so many symptoms in common? Was there a scientific basis for what Selye began to think of as "the syndrome of just being sick" (Selye, 1956, p.16)? What also bothered Selye was the idea that if there was a such a syndrome, why did doctors always concentrate their efforts on specific illnesses and their accompanying treatments without paying any attention to the idea of "just being sick" (Selye, 1956, p.16). This idea and the questions it raised was, for a time, to lose it's meaning as other more pressing requirements required Selye's attention.

Not until 10 years later, in 1935, did the same question again confront Selye and his colleague McKeown. At that time it became apparent from their experimental work that they had isolated a wholly non-specific phenomenon, but because of other competing research interests, they initially found it of little interest. Nevertheless, in an effort to interpret this phenomenon, Selye and McKeown concluded that it was probably best to view it as some sort of expression of "non-specific stress" (Selye, 1952). This was the first time that the term "stress" was used to explain the presence of this non-specific state. Yet this work and this use of the term "stress" were basically ignored by other researchers. This is hardly surprising as the work was described in the appendix of a paper entitled "Studies in the physiology of the maternal placenta in the rat" (Selye and McKeown, 1935). A title hardly suitable as Selye (1952) admits, to call attention to the idea of 'non-specific stress.' However, what was to become his "stress theory" and his use of the term "stress" lay in a different route.

It was a little later in 1935 that Selye was again confronted by the problem of stress. With his hopes dashed at being able to identify a new sex hormone, he was led to revisit his earlier findings. If there was Selye suggested, some sort of non-specific response of the body to any type of change then this may make a valuable study in its own right. Now, to Selye, the unraveling of such a response appeared to be far more important than the discovery of yet another sex hormone. It was this thought that was to remind Selye of his early idea of a "syndrome of just being sick." The result was that Selye's decided to "spend the rest of my life studying this non-specific response" (1952, p.29). A decision, Selye adds, he has never had any reason to regret. Consequently, the outline of the "General Adaptation Syndrome" first appeared in *Nature* in 1936. The publication of this paper should not, however, be associated with the term "stress," as its use by Selye followed a more confused and circuitous route. Selye states that adverse public opinion and too much criticism of his use of the word "stress" led him to temporarily abandon it. What Selye didn't want, was to become embroiled in some sort of "semantic squabble" that would, in his view, obscure the real issue and so he thought that terms like "nocuous" or "noxious" would be considered less disagreeable until the "stress" concept could become better understood (Selye, 1952, p.33).

What is noticeable about Selye's prewar mainstream articles is that none of them made any reference to "stress" (Newton, 1995). So, if Selye had not really published anything on stress prior to the war, then where did all this criticism of his use of the term come from? It seems that this criticism came repeatedly from the debate that followed in the discussion periods after his lectures (Selye, 1952). To Selye, the use of the term "nocuous agent" did not really capture the essence of what he thought of as "stress" and so he was left searching for a more precise meaning. Selye kept turning back to the term "stress," and drawing on an engineering analogy suggested that to him the non-specific response was the biologic equal of what has been called "stress" in inanimate objects. Perhaps, he suggested, one could best describe this response as "biologic stress" (Selye, 1952, p.39).

Lecture discussions criticized Selye's used of the term "stress" in two main ways. The first criticism concerned the use a word like "stress," when it would be more straightforward to use "cold," if, for example, cold was the stimulant that had been used to evoke the non-specific response. The second criticism was simply that if the existence of stress was generally accepted, it would probably not be possible to study it scientifically (Selye, 1952). These criticisms were batted away by Selye, in the belief that they represented a failure to grasp the real nature of the concept of "stress." However, during those early years, few were convinced by his arguments. Steadily, however, more through custom rather than reason, the term quietly entered into every-day language simply because the concept itself was becoming an accepted subject for research. So, although by 1935 Selye had set out the components describing the general adaptational syn-drome, the use of the word "stress" and an outline of his stress theory did not appear until after the war. It seems "that the war was critical to public acceptance of the relevance of stress as a legitimate explanatory concept" (Newton, 1995, p.24) rather than Selye's writings. It was after the war that debate and con-troversy began to surround Selye's work. It is to this period that we now turn.

The postwar interest in stress appears more likely to reflect "military concerns during the war" (Newton, 1995, p.31) rather than what had gone on before. The refocusing of attention on war neuroses, intertwined with increased talk of "nervous tension" and "war nerves" soon became shorthand for "stresses of war." From here it was just a small step to talk about "reactions to stress," and in this way the word simply became part of every-day language. Getting into the habit of using the word "stress" was "seemingly 'learnt' during the war" (Newton, 1995, p.24). The nature of war work also meant that psychologists were in great demand. In the United States, psychology was listed as a critical profession by the War Department (Leahey, 1992), and the influence of psychology during and after the war grew to the point "where it seemed that the United States was becoming a psychological society" (Leahey, 1992, p.39). It wasn't long before "psychologists began to introduce the tools of their trade in an effort to ascertain *who* was under stress and by how much" (Appley and Trumbull, 1986, p.7). The war clearly gave a "renewed impetus to research and theorizing in the area of stress" (Bartlett, 1998, p.28). However, despite the expansion of stress into the social sciences, Selye's work still had a fairly controversial postwar role to play.

General Adaptation Syndrome

Selye "does not outline any stress theory until immediately after the war" (Newton, 1995, p.24). In a paper published in 1946, Selye "elaborates both his concepts concerning 'stress' and the 'General Adaptation Syndrome'" (Mason, 1975a, p.9). Because of the intense debate that was to follow his work, it is worth looking first at the General Adaptation Syndrome, then at his understanding of the nature of stress, before turning to the critical reaction that was never very far from his work. Selye argued that physiological responses to noxious agents or stressors were all part of a coordinated pattern of protection he called the "General Adaptation Syndrome" (GAS). Selye (1956) proposed three stages in its operation: "alarm," "resistance," and "exhaustion." Selye suggested the name "alarm reaction" for the initial response because it most likely represented the body's "call to arms" of its defense systems (Selye, 1982, p.10). If exposure persists beyond the alarm reaction then this is followed by the "stage of resistance." This process of resistance accompanied by various forms of tissue damage was referred to by Selye (1956) as the "diseases of adaptation." Continued resistance led to the depletion of "adaptive energy" and ultimately to the stage of exhaustion and death.

Selye explained that he "called this syndrome *general*, because it is produced only by agents which have a general effect upon large portions of the body. I called it *adaptive*, because it stimulates defense. I called it a *syndrome* because its individual manifestations are coordinated and even partly dependent upon each other" (Selye, 1956, p.32). The nature of the General Adaptation Syndrome raised a number of issues that were as much of a concern to Selye as they were to other researchers who considered his work. They include what is the concept of "stress" being used to describe, what is the distinction between specific and non-specific responses, what triggers the alarm reaction, and what is adaptational energy. Selye argued, that many aspects of the syndrome gradually acquired some sort of meaning almost as they were being observed, and so, because of the need to detail this process it was necessary to give the different elements names. Selye (1956) justified this approach by arguing that while it may seem out of the ordinary to name something before you had a precise understanding of what it was, this was simply the way in exploratory research, because as concepts begin to take shape so do they begin to inherit meaning.

All of these issues will be discussed again when we explore what Selye meant by "stress" and the controversy surrounding his work. At this point it is only necessary to turn our attention to the issue of "adaptive energy." Selye (1982) suggested that the

General Adaptation Syndrome gave the first indication that the body's adaptive energy is finite. More importantly, he added, that we don't really know what adaptive energy is other than it is a fundamental aspect of living (Selye, 1956) and we don't really know what is actually being depleted (Selye, 1982). Sooner or later, Selye (1982) speculated, the "human machine" simply becomes a casualty of continuous wear and tear and such energy should be used prudently and carefully rather then wasted. To his critics the more important question was whether adaptation "is only possibly with the assistance of some sort of energy?" (Doublet, 2000, p.115).

How did Selye's concept of stress evolve? Having established the main features of the General Adaptation Syndrome, Selye was somewhat at a loss as to what produced it, and with no precise idea of what it was he had found, it was difficult to give it a name let alone define it. At first Selye (1956) spoke of "nocuous agents," but even this term did not really capture the nature of what he thought was going on. In his 1946 paper, Selye "used the term 'stress' in the conventional sense of stimuli, evocative agents or *outside forces acting on the organism*" (Mason, 1975a, p.9). At another time looking back over his work, Selye (1976a) suggested, that the "nocuous agents" should, more appropriately, refer to "stressors" since they were, what placed the demand on the system in the first place. If, Selye argued, we distinguished between the specific effects of "nocuous agents" and their common "biologic response" then this may be the key to understanding what we mean by "biologic stress" (Selye, 1976a). He coupled this idea with the notion that "biological stress" is linked to, but not identical with, energy utilization. Selye was also to give new sense to the word "stress," proposing that it be defined as a condition *"within the organism in response to evocative agents"* (Mason, 1975a, p.9). For such evocative agents he again proposed the term "stressors."

A clue as to why Selye continued to modify what he meant by "stress" comes from his view that "in biology, definitions can only serve as concise descriptions of the way we perceive phenomena. And we must keep in mind that at any time our concepts may be modified by further observations" (Selye, 1956, p.53). An operational definition emerged as "stress is the state manifested by a specific syndrome which consists of all the non specifically induced changes within a biologic system"

(Selye 1956, p.54). Eventually what emerged was the idea that stress is fundamentally a physiological response and should be defined as "the sum of all non-specific changes caused by function or damage" (Mason, 1975a, p.10). By 1979, Selye argued that stress could be defined in a variety of ways, giving as one example the wear and tear on the body resulting from any sort of demanding experience. However, in most of his more recent papers, he simply defined it as the body's non-specific response to any demand (Selye, 1979). This definition differed from earlier definitions only in the use of more inclusive language to allow for the growing list of evocative agents or stressors (Mason, 1975a) that were eventually to include psychological, physical, or chemical agents (Tache, 1979).

Yet, as Mason points out, "it is somewhat difficult to trace the evolution of Selye's own thinking processes about the use of the term 'stress.'" At different periods "Selye was inclined towards defining 'stress' variously in terms of either *stimulus, response or interaction between stimulus and response*" (1975a, p.9). In response to this point Selye (1975) indicated that what he was trying to do was to emphasize that stress, defined in terms of his non-specific syndrome, was the result of these interactions. He went on to add that if we continue to make the distinction between "stress" (the non-specific syndrome) and "stressor" (that which caused it) the exact meaning is immediately evident (Selye, 1975). But is it? Is, for example, "stress," the non-specific syndrome, the same response as the General Adaptation Syndrome? Do we have a cascade of syndromes? Ultimately, suggests Doublet, "we are still left to wonder whether the General Adaptation Syndrome and stress describe the same thing" and there appears to be no "adequate explanation of the respective roles of stress and the General Adaptation Syndrome" (2000, p.106).

The essence of stress in Selye's view lay in its non-specificity. The difference between a specific and non-specific response is explained in this way. Selye (1977) first explained that when it comes to stress there are both specific factors and general non-specific ones. He then went on to add that no matter what type of specific effect was produced, all demands have one thing in common; they produce a requirement for adaptation. It is, he emphasized, this requirement for adaptation that is non-specific. It occurs across all demands irrespective of what those demands may be. It then simply becomes, as Selye (1977) notes, a matter of emphasis as to whether one researches the specific or non-specific effects of stressors.

Eustress, Distresss, Hyperstress, and Hypostress

Selye suggested that stress had four basic variations: good stress (*eustress*), bad stress (*distress*), overstress (*hyperstress*), and understress (*hypostress*). He went on to add that the essential purpose of a biologic code of behavior is to arrive at a balance between the negative influences of stress finding as much eustress as possible (Selye, 1979b). This was not the first time Selye talked about the notion of balance and re-establishing normalcy. Drawing on the work of Bernard and Cannon, Selye had used the term "homeostasis" to describe the staying power of the body (Selye, 1956). The question that began to take shape in Selye's mind was, if all demands have these non-specific qualities, could the fight to maintain balance be one of them (Selye, 1956). Could, Selye pondered, our body's have an in-built "non-specific defense system" designed to fight any sort of demand (Selye, 1956). These views "made it possible to understand the biological purpose" of the General Adaptation Syndrome and "at last the non-specific reactions made sense as the body's attempt to maintain a steady state in the face of stress" (Johnson, 1991, p.41). In contrast to the body as a machine idea, under the homeostasis metaphor a "general response makes perfectly good sense, as a self-generated way of maintaining balance within the organism" (Johnson, 1991, p.42). Without the idea of homeostasis, there would be no "motivation for this line of enquiry" (Johnson, 1991, p.42) and the idea of a non-specific response would simply not make sense. Nevertheless the idea of a non-specific response was to arouse considerable debate and controversy.

In spite of the many productive consequences of Selye's work "his theories concerning stress and 'diseases of adaptation' continued to meet with a great deal of critical reaction" (Mason, 1975a, p.10). In the beginning the controversy over Selye's ideas was "waged by argument rather than by experiment" (Mason, 1971, p.323). Two things were to change this. The first was the refinement in methods, making possible remarkable precise and sensitive measurements of physiological changes in the body. The second was the challenge to Selye's ideas from researchers working in the field of psychology. As with many ideas when confronted by new methods and different perspectives "once looked at carefully enough, the simple relationship that Selye predicted tended not to be so simple or predictable at all" (Appley and Trumbull, 1986, p.5). There are, suggests Mason, two features of Selye's formulations which deserve special critical scrutiny not just because they continue to be a source of confusion but because "they are of pivotal importance in judging the validity of Selye's unique concepts of stress" (1975b, p.12). These two features are: that stress is a physiological response within the organism and the validity of the concept of a physiological non-specific response within the organism common to any demand.

In terms of the first feature – that stress is a physiological response within the organism – two issues are involved. These include: (a) what is the nature of the alarm reaction, and (b) does psychology have a role to play and, if so, how? In his autobiography Selye (1979), credited Cannon more than any other, as providing a great source of inspiration especially his discovery of the fight or flight response. Selye (1956) seems to suggest that the alarm reaction stage of the General Adaptation Syndrome could be a case of flight or fight or as the prompt that sets off the alarm. However, by 1976, Selye seems to be questioning the utility of the flight or fight response by suggesting that this basically practical evolutionary developed defense, could if inappropriately triggered, be a primary cause of disease. His colleague Tache (1979) was to make this point even clearer by stating that "this biological vestige is mobilized too often in circumstances where it need not be, given the high price it exacts in terms of health and well-being" (1979, p.9). Selye intended the alarm reaction to reflect both a "call to arms" and a defensive mobilization that can increase susceptibility to all illness. Both are present in his writing and his diseases of adaptation appeared to be basically initiated by the body itself because of its inappropriate response to a potentially harmful demand (Selye, 1973). Selye's idea that disease may be due to the maladaptive response of the body was to some writers "of the highest significance" because this knowledge would allow Selye's work to be applied to helping people gain "full control over their physical and mental processes" (Le Vay, 1952, p.168). Nevertheless, it is perhaps ironic, that he could never convince

Cannon that his most fundamental contribution to the field was that there was both a specific and a non-specific response of the body (Selye, 1979).

Yet, it was not so much the nature of the alarm reaction, but the search for what actually triggered it, that illustrated the role that psychology was to play in unraveling the stress process and establishing the direction for future research. In 1956, Selye indicated, that step-by-step, the principal elements of the General Adaptation Syndrome had been documented and defined, but he still had little idea as to what produced it. In Selye's mind, the most serious obstacle in the study of stress is a complete lack of knowledge about the nature of these alarm signals. Selye named these alarm signals or messengers "first mediators" (see 1976a, p.24). In his 1976a review, Selye admitted being puzzled by the nature of the first mediator, which he saw as the carrier of the stress message from the area of exposure to the mechanisms that control homeostatic adjustment. Selye's search was always for some physiological first mediators either in terms of "some chemical by-product of activity" or "lack of some important blood constituent that cells use" (Selye, 1976, p.56).

Yet his search proved fruitless, and he was left exclaiming that one of the important goals for future stress researchers was to identify the *nature* of the first mediator (Selye, 1976). It was a new line of approach that was to be more productive. "The unrecognized first mediator in many of Selye's experiments simply may have been the psychological apparatus involved in emotional arousal" (Mason, 1975b, p.25). The challenge from psychology had begun. Lazarus (1977), for example, argued that Selye had failed to take into account the "psychological signalling system" (p.17) that distinguishes noxious events from benign ones. Similarly, Monat and Lazarus (1991) were to suggest that it was more likely that the body's responses are set in motion as a result of how the demand was appraised. There was, Lazarus (1977) argued, limited but challenging empirical evidence that the crucial first mediator of the GAS could be psychological. Selye (1975; 1979a) was to remain unconvinced.

It was Mason who was also to question the generality of the non-specific response. It is, suggested Mason, a matter of enormous magnitude "to establish experimentally the validity of a concept of total or absolute non-specificity for a bodily response as being 'common to all types of exposure'" (1975b, p.30).

Mason's findings that in response to different stressors there may be an increase, decrease, or no effect on physiological functioning led to the conclusion that Selye may have overstated the generality of the stress response. Doublet, in his review of Selye's work, also drew attention to the fact that "as research is discovering more systems that participate in stress responses, it has become increasingly unclear whether after removing these specific reactions any truly non-specific reactions would eventually remain" (2000, p.119).

Selye (1976) would not be shifted from the non-specific response but would seemingly concede that the way in which a demand is perceived, may be dependent not just on its intensity but also on the vulnerability of the individual. He also seemed to touch on the idea of coping by pointing out that individual actions may also influence the non-specific effects of the demand (Selye, 1976). To Selye (1973) though, variations in the non-specific response could simply be accounted for by what he described as "conditioning factors" (p.696) that have the ability to influence the effects of stress and, in this way, to Selye the integrity of the non-specific response was maintained. This was probably Selye's way of acknowledging the issue of individual differences in functioning and the different nature of stressors but stopping short of actually accounting for them (Cassidy, 1999).

Physiological Aspects of Stress

Mason's critique of Selye's concept of stress was in many ways a response to a tendency by other researchers to vaguely assume that there were close linkages between the emerging interest in the psychological aspects of stress and the work of Selye. This was not, of course, the case as the interest in stress from a psychological point of view had developed quite separately from Selye's work. Nevertheless, in evaluating Selye's work it is clear when addressing the question of what are the substantive linkage between Selye's stress concepts, "derived from primarily physiological research," and the stress concepts developed in "largely independent fashion in the psychological stress field" (Mason, 1975b, p.22), the answer is none. Selye's work was "entrenched in the biological" (Martin, 1984, p.448), and remained fundamentally physiological. Selye wrote that when he first began his work on "stress" he "gave little thought to its psychological or sociological implications for I saw stress as a purely physiological and medical phenomenon" (Selye, 1983, p.1). He then went on to add that the growing interest in psychological stress made him realize that an understanding of stress would profit everybody, but this did not seem to constitute any sort of explanation of whether psychology had a role to play in his work. "Selye's various pronouncements," as Doublet suggests, "render the task of understanding where he stood with regard to psychological stress somewhat difficult" (2000, p.109).

As researchers in the field began to focus more and more on the psychological aspects of stress, it is clear that Selye "attempted to generalize many of his findings about physical factors to psychological factors" (Doublet, 2000, p.108), using in his definitions of stress an "all-inclusive phraseology" to capture the range of "evocative agents" (Mason, 1975a, p.10). But while Selye was writing "Stressors, it should be noted are not exclusively physical in nature" followed by "psychological arousal is one of the most frequent activators," (1982, p.14), he was, at the same time, writing about why he was not be able to "accept emotional arousal as the common cause of stress responses" (Selye, 1979a, p.15). The best conclusion that can be drawn from all this is that "Selye is nowhere basing his ideas on psychological experiments" (Martin, 1984, p.448). He talks, as Martin goes on to point out, about "psychological stress as if it were allied to his own earlier writings. This is an extrapolation which is not justified." To include psychological stimuli in Selye's work "is an expanded view of stress which requires elucidation beyond what this outstanding researcher has explored" (Martin, 1984, p.448).

It is important to let Selye have the last word. "As I see it" he wrote, "man's ultimate aim is to *express himself* [sic] *as fully as possible according to his own lights*" (Selye, 1956, p.299). We need a "natural code of ethics" (Selye, 1974), behaviors that act as guidelines that are compatible with scientific laws governing homeostasis and that provide the opportunity to live in equilibrium and harmony with our surroundings. The "meaning of my life has been to convey, not just to my colleagues in medical science but to the general public, what I have learnt through my research – how we can live with stress and make it work for us" (Selye,

1979, p.266). This "is the greatest obligation of science to humanity" (Selye, 1979a, p.29).

The Work of Harold Wolff

Selye's work spanned six decades and during the period of his work several other developments were to influence the course of stress research. One such influence was Harold Wolff (1953), who expounded "the idea that life stress played a role in the aetiology of disease" (Bartlett, 1998, p.27). In his book *Stress and Disease*, Wolff (1953) wrote "the common knowledge that man [*sic*] gets sick when life circumstances are adverse, and is healthy when they are propitious has been here extended by precise measurements of bodily functions before, during and after periods of stress." Wolff went on to state "It is shown how the impact of man [*sic*] on man may be as seriously traumatic as the assaults of micro-organisms climate, chemical and physical forces" (p.vi). Wolff's work was to carry one step further Bernard's concept of disease, where Bernard described disease "as the outcome of attempts at homeostasis in which adaptive responses to noxious forces, although appropriate in kind, were faulty in amount" (Wolff, 1953, p.vi). Wolff was to suggest that individuals, when faced with a threat, especially one involving values and beliefs "initiate responses inappropriate in kind as well as in magnitude. Such reactions, integrated for one protective purpose, and thus inappropriately used for another, can damage or destroy" (1953 p.vii).

The Protective Reaction

Wolff's work is often overlooked, or given only the very briefest of mentions, when the history of stress is discussed. This is odd as his work is rich in meaning. It reflects an amalgam of ideas that captures the spirit of the time, the social reformist ideals of psychosomatic medicine, the debate about how stress should be defined, the role that society and psychology may play in explaining the stress process, and the preventive and therapeutic strategies that could be developed to fulfill needs, realize aspirations, and develop potential. The key concept in Wolff's work was the "protective reaction response." This response described by reviewers as corresponding to "to the process of mobilizing resources" (Howard and Scott, 1965, p.155), reflects the view that when confronted with physical agents or symbolic dangers or threats the body sets in motion a complex set of reactions aimed at getting rid of the threat. The reaction to physical and symbolic threats is the same. In contrast to the work of Selye, protective reactions "are not 'chain' reactions in which the individual first feels followed by altered bodily function" (Wolff, 1953, p.9), but are "considered to occur simultaneously and in varying degrees" (Howard and Scott, 1965, p.155). The central thesis in Wolff's work is, as noted above, that individuals continually "over-mobilise [their] physical resources when confronted with problems originating in the symbolic environments, and that to the extent that these problems remain unresolved, a state of inappropriate mobilization is perpetuated" (Howard and Scott, 1965, p.155).

Much of what was to evolve into the relationship between life experiences and stress is present in Wolff's view that in any situation stress is largely the result of the way in which that situation is perceived, and that this perception depends upon a wide variety of factors including the "generic equipment, basic individual needs and longings, earlier conditioning influences, and a host of life experiences and culture pressures" (1953, p.10). Yet all the time Wolff draws one back to the idea that what a person does in relation to a threat is frequently out of keeping with what he or she ought to do. The result is that the "responses which result in disease may be qualitatively [in kind] as well as quantitatively [in amount] inappropriate." The protective reaction that serves one purpose (bacterial invasion) when used to serve another (interpersonal conflict), may be inappropriately used and "since resolution cannot be effected through its use, the unsuitability of the reaction pattern as well as its magnitude and duration, especially endanger survival" (Wolff, 1953, p.150). The question of when is the protective reaction response appropriate or inappropriate must, as Hinkle suggests (1973), become a matter of judgment. In order to make that judgment, researchers are faced with answering the question "appropriate to whom and at what cost?" To Wolff, "Whether appropriately or inappropriately used, adaptive and protective patterns operate only in relation to the present, in a manner determined by the past, and often with dangerous consequences for the future" (1953, p.150). Wolff's protection reaction response has also been criticized because "the major problem with this model" is it doesn't explain why individuals respond in different ways to noxious symbolic stimuli (Scott and Howard, 1970, p.268). In the end, Wolff makes it clear that individuals must appreciate what their actions are costing them. Costs may include pain and illness. However Wolff's (1953) hope is that every individual will decide that what is required is a change in direction and pace and thus a change in health.

It would be tempting to make all sorts of connections between Wolff's work and much of the stress research that was to follow. There are, in addition to biological and physiological elements in his work aspects of sociology, psychology, and a platform from which the self-help movement was to grow. But Wolff's view of stress, despite his references to "symbolic threats," and the emphasis he placed on daily living, and the goals of individuals and their culture, was to remain essentially that " 'stress' is a 'state' within the organism" (Hinkle, 1973, p.35). Wolff argued, "if the word 'stress' was to enter the language of biological science, responsibilities concerning its meaning are entailed" (1953, p.v). Wolff discharged his responsibilities by stating "as it has been defined in mechanics, 'stress' is the internal or resisting force brought into action in parts by external forces or loads [stimuli]" and so "*stress* becomes the *interaction* between external environment and organism, with the past experience of the organism as a major factor" (1953, p.v). Wolff was to eventually write, "Since stress is a dynamic state within an organism in response to a demand for adaptation, and since life itself entails constant adaptation, living creatures are continually in a state of more or less stress" (Hinkle, 1973, p.35).

Although Wolff "had not entirely freed himself from the simpler analogies" (Hinkle, 1973, p.45) that reflected his views on stress, it was evident he had become aware of the communicative nature of the relationship between organisms and their environment helping to dispel what, up to then, had been a "rather uncritical assumption that there is a linear relation between events outside of the organism and events within the organism" (Hinkle, 1973, p.45). His work also led others to consider the degree of stressfulness of events in the social environment. In short, the observations of Wolff and others writing about stress "in the 1940s and 1950s have not only been supported by subsequent knowledge, but have been vastly extended" (Hinkle, 1973, p.45).

Summary

The physiological approach to understanding stress made an enormous impact on stress research. The work of researchers like Cannon, Selye, and Wolff spanned almost 80 years, and although it is possible to identify milestones in their writings and to use these to describe the contribution they made, such milestones should not be assumed to be discrete events. They represent just one point, although a very significant one, in decades of discussion, debate, and controversy. When considering the work of these researchers we are immediately confronted by the issue "what to include?" Our aim has been to trace a set of ideas, events, and people that aids our understanding of how we got to be where we are now. Our objective, depending on the event or issue under consideration, has been to "use history to understand" (Leahey, 1992, p.35). We have attempted to present events and issues in a way that captures the spirit of the times, trying not to let our present understanding of those events color the way those events are presented too much. What we don't want to do, is present a way of thinking about events as being "strictly cumulative, one finding building on another as more information about the phenomenon is accumulated" (Bartlett, 1998, p.23). So, in summarizing the state of stress research up until the 1950s and 1960s, the issues about to be discussed may provide a context for understanding where we are and the forces that began to introduce further change.

It is important to emphasize that stress research developed "historically in two largely separate spheres [physiology and psychology]" (Mason, 1975a, p.22). It is "an interesting historical paradox" argues Mason, "that, 20 years ago psychological variables generally were regarded by physiologists as negligible experimental factors in comparison with such 'substantial' physical variables as heat, cold, exercise, trauma and so on" (1975a, p.24). So, each field developed in an autonomous fashion. The transition from the physiological work of researchers like Cannon and Selye to psychological approaches to understanding stress "is often portrayed in terms of the former providing an impetus for the latter in a continuous flow of ideas" but this is incorrect as "there is actually discontinuity in moving from one to the other" (Bartlett, 1998, p.27). The first psychological approaches to understanding stress were spawned almost independently of the work of Cannon and Selye. Although the connection between the two has been described as somewhat fundamental and their separation artificial (Singer and Davidson, 1986), the truth is that each developed in a rather independent way. The fact that psychological processes were later used as a route for understanding physiological reactions, should not be taken as representing an orderly transition from one discipline to the other.

Looking back over the first 50 years of research into stress and disease there is a consensus among reviewers that the substance of the work developed by Cannon, Selye, and Wolff "appears to be correct, and it is generally accepted to be so" (Hinkle, 1987, p.566). Their view that the onset of disease appears to be "a phenomenon that occurs when an agent or condition threatens to destroy the dynamic state upon which the integrity of the organism depends" (Hinkle, 1987, p.566) appears to be thoroughly established. In this sense, as Selye described them, all diseases can be considered as diseases of adaptation. Accepting the fundamental importance of the idea of equilibrium has not, of course, prevented researchers from debating its nature (see, for example, Howard and Scott, 1965). However, the explanation provided by these early researchers as to how stress caused disease based around the engineering notion of a a state of stress within the organism "is clearly wrong," (Hinkle, 1987, p.566) failing as it does to take into account the communicative interaction between the organism and the environment. The idea that any response to a threat was based around appraising information raised a range of questions about how stress causes diseases and a sense that such questions seemed "to be waiting for social scientists to have a look at them" (Hinkle, 1987, p.566).

The biological study of stress following the work of Selye "began to focus on a more detailed analysis of the physiological processes and developed into the modern field of psychoneuroimmunology" (Cassidy, 1999, p.24). Psychoneuroimmunology (PNI) is "the study of the interrelations between the central nervous system and the immune system" (Cohen and Herbert,

1996, p.114). The popularity of this field stems from its promise "to explore and explain the common belief that our personalities and emotions influence our health" (Cohen and Herbert, 1996, p.114). A central tenet of psychoneuroimmunology is that when the immune system is weakened, we are vulnerable to a range of illnesses and "that stress impacts on the immune system to weaken its function" (Cassidy, 1999, p.24). Reviewers of this field talk in terms of "psychologically and biologically plausible explanations" and "consistent and convincing evidence [at least in the case of less serious infectious diseases] between stress and disease onset and progression," yet what is missing "is strong evidence that the association between psychological factors and disease that do exist are attributable to immune changes" (Cohen and Herbert, 1996, p.136).

The road towards forging such links is "littered with formidable obstacles" (Evans, Clow, and Hucklebridge, 1997, p.303) not the least of which include defining stress or gauging the state of the immune system. The fact that this field continues to raise intriguing questions means that researchers must "remain alive to the possibility that severe and chronic stress may well have more serious effects on both the immune system and physical health," and so it remains for PNI researchers "to get on with the sober business of collecting and examining the scientific evidence" (Evans et al., 1997, p.306 and p.304). Intricately woven in all this are psychological and emotional processes, demanding external events, and individual vulnerability. Yet to understand the role of psychology in stress research and the directions it has taken there is another whole history that must be explored. Psychoneuroimmunology owes as much to this history as it does to the founding work of Cannon, Selye, and Wolff.

CHAPTER THREE

The Twentieth Century: From the 1950s to Richard Lazarus

Introduction: Stress in the 1950s and 1960s

By the end of the 1950s, "stress as a legitimate subject of academic study had arrived" (Newton, 1995, p.31). By this time the stress concept had also become established within the discipline of psychology. But, even at this stage, as a relative newcomer to psychology, concerns were being voiced at whether stress was just another fad, and like other fads bringing with it "an enthusiasm not altogether commensurate with their value to our science as a whole" and with emotional overtones "sometimes apt to blind protagonists to the deficiencies which exist in most new ideas" (Haward, 1960, p.185). Giving rise to this early speculation as to whether stress was just a fad was an even more fundamental concern that was, and is, still being played out. Then, as now, this concern found expression in stress "the term," rather than stress "the concept," and the ostensibly careless approach to defining it' coupled with the inconsistent ways in which the term was being used. The history of stress in the second half of the twentieth century is no less controversial than the 50 years of debate and discussion that preceded it.

"However vacuous or not," the term stress "has taken a tenacious hold on our society and is likely to be around for some time to come" (Jones and Bright, 2001, p.12). The elasticity in its meaning provided an opportunity to consider stress from a number of perspectives. Developments throughout this period meant that attempts to provide any coherent theoretical framework required that different perspectives be identified, tested, reviewed, integrated, or even discarded. As researchers gained confidence in researching the concept, identifying the strength and weaknesses of different perspectives and searching for common features that would provide an organizing context, the history of stress spills out into a history of traditions and themes, of distinctive approaches, of paradigm shifts, and of practical concerns and appropriate methods. "What is a 'popular' area of research, at any given time is not at all a random matter. There is often a theoretic and methodological history leading up to the point at which a research topic blossoms; and there is usually a contemporaneous *zeitgeist* containing forces conducive to that blossoming" (McGrath, 1970, p.2). The blossoming of stress research is captured in the history that follows.

If the history of stress is a history of distinctive approaches, then the history of stress is also, to a very large measure, a history of psychosomatic medicine. In the 1960s and 1970s psychosomatic theories took as a goal, to explore those psychosocial variables which increase vulnerability to illness as well as those which support adaptive coping with it (Lipowski, 1977a). This goal provided the fertile ground for much of the early work on life events, life changes, and stressors. But psychosomatic medicine had already left its mark on the concept of stress, inspired by the force of psychoanalytic theory. Although by the 1950s the influence of these theories "suffered a sharp drop in popularity and credibility and seemed to be heading for the annals of medical history" (Lipowski, 1977a, p.235), they are part of the history of stress and are mentioned here to give a sense of completion. Perhaps the most influential representative of this psychodynamic approach was Alexander.

Alexander's "specificity theory" linked unresolved unconscious conflicts that "engendered chronic emotional tensions" with "specific somatic disorders" (Lipowski, 1977a, p.235). Alexander applied his theory to several "chronic diseases of unknown etiology" such as, for example, hypertension and peptic ulcer (Lipowski, 1986a, p.3). These diseases soon became known as "psychosomatic disorders." His theory came to dominate psychosomatic medicine for around 25 years until the mid 1950s. However, his 'specificity hypothesis' proved extremely difficult to validate, simplified what were complex causal links, and failed to bring about the hoped-for "treatment results." This approach simply "ground to a halt" leaving behind a feeling of "widespread disenchantment" (Lipowski, 1977a, p.235). The field survived this crisis with a change in emphasis from the increasingly narrow preoccupation with psychodynamics, to a much broader approach both in scope and method concerned with the bio-psycho-social determinants of health and disease.

It is difficult to give an overview of a field like psychosomatic medicine "that is so broad, diversified and vigorously evolving" (Lipowski, 1977a, p.233). The field is much more than a scientific discipline (Lipowski, 1977a; 1986b). It sees the individual as "ceaselessly interacting with the social and physical environment in which they are embedded" and its role as a reformist movement that advocates a more complex, holistic, and systems view of the individual that straddles "interdisciplinary boundaries" (Lipowski, 1977a pp.235, 236). It asks a number of "deceptively simple questions" that center on the kinds of social situations, the characteristics of individuals, the coping strategies they adopt, and those pathways and mechanisms that help to explain "why a person responds to particular social situations and specific life events with a given pattern of psychological and physiological changes" (Lipowski, 1977a, p.236). The revival of the field in the 1960s posed a number of challenges for researchers that focused on two main issues. The first was the causal relationship between life events and illness whilst the second concerned the role of individual difference and personality variables in illness (Lipowski, 1986c). These issues are part and parcel of the history of stress and reflect the new phase that stress research was to enter into (Lipowski, 1986b).

Stressful Life Events

Almost all introductions to stressful life events begin by acknowledging the work of Selye. "Recognition of the generality of the stress process as suggested by Selye," notes Cassidy, "led a number of psychiatrists in the psychosomatic tradition to look at the relationship between life events and psychiatric disorders" (1999, p.38). Dohrenwend (1979) described the importance of stressful life event research by first making the point that, "life events are eminently researchable," and followed it up with the view that "they are important to the people we study, things that they are interested in and can tell us about" and then concluded "if environmentally induced stress is an important factor in psychopathology in the general population, then life events are strategic phenomena on which to focus as major sources of such stress" (p.11). Systematic research on stressful life events grew mainly from the seminal work of Cannon, Wolff, and Meyer. It was "Cannon's experimental work" that "provided a necessary link in the argument that stressful life events can be harmful. That is, he showed that stimuli associated with emotional arousal cause changes in basic physiological processes" (Dohrenwend and Dohrenwend, 1974a, p.3).

Wolff (1950) also provided a stimulus for more systematic research into stressful life events, following his review of the proceedings of the *Association for Research in Nervous and Mental Disease Conference* in 1949 on "Life Stress and Bodily Disease." The extent of the research that had accumulated by then on the effects of stressful life events and the range of diseases covered (Wolff, Wolf, and Hare, 1950) led Wolff to conclude, "The common denominator in psychosomatic illness is the interpretation of an event as threatening. This implies anxiety, conscious or unconscious and the need to formulate a protective reaction pattern" (1950, p.1090). "These threats and conflicts," Wolff noted, "are omnipresent, and constitute a large section of stress to which man [sic] is exposed" (1950, p.1059). These threats are reacted to by the mobilization of an individuals defenses. Wolff, in trying to explain the impact of life stress that had, by then, become evident, identified three propositions aimed at taking life event research forward (Dohrenwend and Dohrenwend, 1974). All three propositions "have proved controversial" (Dohrenwend and Dohrenwend, 1974a, p.4) but it was the first, more generic statement, indicating that irrespective of its scale, the potential of a given event to evoke a protective reaction is dependent on its significance to that person (Wolff, 1950) which was to become "central to subsequent research on stressful life events" (Dohrenwend and Dohrenwend, 1974a, p.4).

If Selye, Cannon, and Wolff were to provide the links between stressful life events and disease then much of life event research "evolved from the chrysalis of psychobiology generated by Adolf Meyer through his invention and use of the 'life chart' " (Holmes and Masuda, 1974, p.45). Meyer's philosophy is captured in the forward to Lief's (1948) biographical narrative on *The Commonsense Psychiatry of Dr. Adolf Meyer*. Meyer argued, "psychiatry has to be found in the function and the life of the people" (Lief, 1948, p.viii). "A patient," he added "was not a mere summing-up of cells and organs, but a human being in need of readjustment to the demands of life.... The physician must now add to the disturbances of part-functions those of person-functions and the story of life.... It is 'the story' that counts in a person" (Lief, 1948, p.x). In his paper on the 'life chart,' Meyer wrote "Medical psychology consists largely in the determination of the actual life history and experiences and concrete reactions of the patient" (1948, p.418). To capture 'the story' Meyer used "a device which, I hope, illustrates not only our practice, but also the entire philosophy involved in it" (Meyer, 1919, p.1129). Onto the life chart after entering date and year of birth "we next enter the periods of disorders of the various organs, and after this the data concerning the situations and reactions of the patients." Meyer goes on to indicate, "we may note the change of habitat... the various 'jobs;' the dates of possibly important births and deaths in the family, and other fundamentally important environmental incidents" (1919, p.1132). Meyer's teaching illustrated the important part that life events play in the onset of disease and his suggestion that even the most usual and ordinary life events are potential contributors to the development of illness, provided, for a number of researchers, the way forward (Dohrenwend and Dohrenwend, 1974). Meyer's life charting technique, and many of the life events he identified, provided for Holmes and Rahe, a framework and context from which they developed *The Social Readjustment Rating Scale* (SRRS) (Holmes and Rahe, 1967). This was one of two paths that life event research was to follow: to explore the accumulated effect of a series of major life events. The other focused on the effect of single events or classes of events.

The Social Readjustment Scale

By the time Holmes and Rahe came to publish their *Social Readjustment Rating Scale* in 1967, the "life chart device had been used systematically with over 5000 patients to study the quality and quantity of life events empirically observed to cluster at the time of disease onset" (1967, p.215). From this pool of events, 43 were identified as reflecting these experiences. The life events used in the SRRS were originally used to construct a *Schedule of Recent Experience* (SRE). The work using the SRE (Rahe, Meyer, Smith, Kjaer, and Holmes, 1964) "had been used to adduce data that the life events cluster significantly in the 2-year period preceding onset of tuberculosis, heart disease, skin disease, hernia and pregnancy" (Holmes and Masuda, 1974, p.57). The development of the SRRS took the SRE a stage further by developing a scale reflecting the magnitude for each life event and so "provided a unique method for validation of the findings of the retrospective studies and for a quantitative definition of a life crisis" (Holmes and Masuda, 1974, p.57).

The 43 events fell into two categories: "those indicative of the *life style* of the individual, and those indicative of *occurrences* involving the individual" (Holmes and Rahe, 1967, p.216, emphasis added). These included, for example, death of a spouse, marriage, change in financial state, change to different line of work, revision of personal habits, and vacation. Interviews during the development phase of the SRRS to capture the meanings individuals gave to events identified one theme common to the life events. The occurrence of each was, for the individual involved, associated with, or required some form of coping behavior (Holmes and Rahe, 1967). Holmes and Rahe were to add, that for each event in the SRRS, the "emphasis is on change from the existing steady state and not on psychological meaning, emotion, or social desirability" (1967, p.217).

The next step in the development of the SRRS was to determine the *magnitude* of the different events. In this stage of the research (Holmes and Masuda, 1974) it was explained to participants that social readjustment referred to the "amount and duration of change in one's accustomed pattern of life resulting from various life events" (Holmes and Masuda, 1974, p.49). Each participant was then asked to rate the events "as to their relative degrees of necessary adjustment" (Holmes and Masuda, 1974, p.49). To give respondents some referent point marriage was given an arbitrary value of 500. Each event was then considered in relation to whether it required more or less adjustment than marriage. The mean score for each event was then divided by 10 to produce a life change unit (LCU) score. A life crisis was, defined "as any clustering of life-change events whose individual values summed to 150 LCU or more in any one year" (Holmes and Masuda, 1974, p.59). Research using the SRRS was to show that the magnitude of life changes was significantly related to the timing of disease onset, and to the seriousness of the illness experienced. This life events approach has, over the last 30 years, generated a huge amount of research and a considerable number of publications. The SRRS or one of its adaptations is frequently found in popular health magazines and self-help books. It "represented a significant leap forward in researchers' ability to measure life events and assess their impacts. However, inevitably the approach has generated a great deal of criticism" (Jones and Kinman, 2001, p.23).

In 1973, Barbara Dohrenwend and Bruce Dohrenwend decided, because of the interest in, and importance of stressful life events, to hold a conference on *Stressful Life Events: Their Nature and Effects*. Their motivation for holding the conference was because they felt "the time was ripe for stock-taking and that a careful and thorough job of it could be not only an immediate help to those working on the problem but also a platform from which major new advances could be launched" (Dohrenwend and Dohrenwend, 1974, p.vi). Their book, published in 1974, resulted directly from this conference, and the trends, problems, and prospects identified in the presentations and discussions covered a number of the criticisms leveled at this approach. The debate that accompanied research into stressful life events ranged over 15 years, and in 1990 the lead article (Lazarus, 1990) and the commentaries that followed in the first edition of the *Psychological Inquiry* (an international journal of peer commentary and review), continued to discuss methodological and conceptual issues surrounding the measurement of stressful life events. The criticism surrounding stressful life events has been wide-ranging and well covered within the literature (see Jones and Kinman, 2001 pp.23–4), for example, the fact that measures failed to discriminate between positive and negative events, ignored chronic or recurrent events, failed to take into account individual differences, questioned the reliability and validity of reporting of events over the space of a year, and asked whether their were moderating variables that influenced the relationship.

The criticism that attracted the most attention, however, surrounded "whether it is the objective presence of life events that should be the focus of interest or the person's appraisal of them as being stressful" (Jones and Kinman, 2001, p.24). This objective-subjective debate reached such a level, that at its peak, one commentator (Deutsch, 1986), called for a "freeze" on what she described as these "stress wars." The debate stemmed from Lazarus and his colleagues (Lazarus, DeLongis, Folkman, and

Gruen, 1985) plea to account for the appraisal of events, which would provide an understanding of the process through which stressful life events may influence health, and Dohrenwend and Shrout (1985) who "urged researchers to measure pure environmental events, uncontaminated by perceptions, appraisals or reactions" (p.782). This debate was somewhat fueled by arguments that it was "daily hassles and uplifts" (Kanner, Coyne, Schaefer, and Lazarus, 1981, p.1) that were a more useful measure than stressful life events because of their "conceptual closeness to the person's experience" (Jones and Kinman, 2001, p.25) and because they were more closely related to illness.

Daily Hassles and Uplifts and the Debate that Followed

Efforts to measure "daily hassles and uplifts" arose out of a concern about the measurement difficulties associated with the SRRS. The debate that was to follow the development of the *Hassles Scale*, may well have had its roots in the fact that the scales authors made it clear that the critical life events' approach left almost completely unexamined, and offered nothing by way of an explanation, as to the *processes* through which life events might influence quite different aspects of health. As a result, the life event approach to stress failed to give any attention to more complex issues, such as the influence of the meaning of the event and the impact of different coping behaviors. Despite "the essential reasonableness of the assumption that the accumulation of life events should be relevant to health status" such "indexes tell us nothing about what actually happens in day-to-day living" (Kanner et al., 1981, p.2). It is these day-to-day events "that ultimately should have proximal significance for health outcomes and whose accumulative impact, therefore, should also be assessed" (Kanner et al., 1981, p.3).

The primary objective in constructing the *Hassles Scale* was to capture a broad range of everyday life difficulties as perceived by the individual, rather than to attempt to generate purely objective environmental events (Lazarus, 1984). Daily hassles were defined as: "experiences and conditions of daily living that have been appraised as salient and harmful to the endorser's well-being" (Lazarus, 1984a, p.376). This definition places hassles firmly as a subjective experience, with the meanings associated with them leading them to be remembered. Scale events (Kanner et al., 1981) generated by the researchers and colleagues, included for example, misplacing and losing things, 'concerns about getting credit, smoking too much, nonfamily members living in your house, not enough money for food, not getting enough sleep, and too many things to do. Daily uplifts, however, were defined, as: "experiences and conditions of daily living that have been appraised as salient and positive or favourable to the endorser's well-being" (Lazarus, 1984a, p.376). Scale events (Kanner et al., 1981) included, for example, being lucky, feeling healthy, being efficient, making a friend, and relaxing. The scale was made up of 117 hassles and 135 uplifts. It was possible using the scales scoring procedures to calculate the frequency, cumulated severity, and intensity of the events. The testing of the scale led the authors to conclude that the pattern of results offer "a surprisingly robust case" that "daily hassles provide a more direct and broader estimate of stress than major life events" and are "more strongly associated with adaptational outcomes than are life events" (Kanner et al., 1981, p.20).

The Debate: Critical Life Events versus Hassles and Uplifts

The lines had been drawn between those favoring a critical life event approach (objective presence of an event) and those arguing for the focus to shift to daily hassles and uplifts (personal appraisal of an event). One issue that separated the two groups was the issue of confounding or overlap between measures. *Confounding* occurs when an event is expressed in such a way, that it may, more likely, be measuring symptoms of illness (e.g. not enough personal energy, concerns about inner conflicts) and so overlap with the measures of illness themselves, thus confusing the measurement of events with the measurement of health outcomes. The debate developed along two lines. The first was to approach the confounding problem by identifying events that had symptom-like properties. For example, Monroe (1983) points to a number of hassles that he describes as "being more directly related to psychological problems or symptoms" (p.191). These he identified as trouble relaxing, trouble making decisions, not getting enough sleep, and too many responsibilities. The debate began in earnest in 1985 with Dohrenwend, Dohrenwend, Dodson, and Shrout attempting to examine more systematically the issue of confounding. Their findings suggested that while there was level of confounding in most scales, critical life events and hassles alike, the issue was more apparent in the *Daily Hassles Scale*. These authors did temper their results with the view that "more care needs to be paid to how they [events] are conceptualized, measured, and employed in the design of research" (Dohrenwend et al., 1985, p.228).

The debate then shifted to the pages of the *American Psychologist*. The response by Lazarus and his colleagues (Lazarus, DeLongis, Folkman, and Gruen, 1985) was quick, robust and clear. In their view the appraisal process simply cannot and should not be separated from the measurement of psychological stress and, therefore, some degree of confounding is unavoidable. It is not possible, they argued, because of the fundamental role of appraisal in the stress process, to simply focus on the environmental aspects of the event, as Dohrenwend et al., (1985) suggested, and make it independent of the stress process. The rejoinder by Dohrenwend and Shrout was just as clear, with their plea to researchers to "measure pure environmental events, uncontaminated by perceptions, appraisals or reaction" (1985, p.782). To Dohrenwend and Shrout the *Hassles Scale* was, in terms of their examination, even more confounded than they had originally thought, even though, they recognized, that the impact of life events would vary depending on individual differences, personal agenda, and available resources. To investigate these issues was, they argued, an important next step. However their advice to Lazarus and his colleagues was unequivocal. "We think, however, that Lazarus and his colleagues would do well to first change their approach to measuring hassles" (Dohrenwend and Shrout, 1985, p.785).

In 1988, DeLongis, Folkman, and Lazarus were to present findings from a thoroughly revised version of the *Hassles and Uplifts Scale*. In the revised version redundant items and words that could be confused with symptoms were all eliminated. The format was also changed so that respondents could rate each item on how much of a hassle or uplift it was for them that day. The revised scale consisted of 53 items. In summarizing the main findings, the authors indicated that an increase in daily hassles tended to be associated with a decline in health (DeLongis *et al.* 1988). Referring to the debate on confounding, DeLongis and colleagues reported that because those items that appear to be confounded with psychological well-being were removed from the present analysis then the suggestion that it was confounding that accounted for the relationship between hassles and health status was indefensible.

The debate was not yet ready to disappear. In his target article in *Psychological Inquiry* in 1990, Lazarus once again made clear that if you adopt the position as he had that stress is always a product of appraisal then inevitability there is going to be some confounding between measures of stress and illness. Again he set out the argument that it was the appraisal process that linked the person and the environment, and so it was just not possible to return to objective environmental events or purifying an event of some contaminating subjective influence. Those commentating on Lazarus's arguments were to suggest otherwise. This time the question of confounding took a different direction. Rather than focusing on item overlap, commentators suggested that confounding arose because the *Daily Hassles Scale* was not so much a measure of "proximal stressors, but an indirect measure of personality" (Costa and McCrae, 1990, p.23), in this case neuroticism. Watson (1990) was also to suggest that the *Daily Hassles Scale* "can be most parsimoniously viewed as a measure of dissatisfaction and emotional distress" (p.34). Furthermore, Costa and McCrae were to suggest, "it is perfectly reasonable to analyze the impact of objective-environmental events, because some events may be presumed to be stressful for most individuals" (1990, p.23).

To the notion that the source of confounding in the *Daily Hassles Scale* is because it is a surrogate measure of some undisclosed personality trait, Lazarus responded that this criticism, may in part be correct, but was somewhat overstated (1990a). Turning the question back on his critics Lazarus (1990a) asked, why must it be some personality trait; why not the other way around, where it is simply the appraisal process that is the appropriate causal link. As to the issue of objective measurement, Lazarus's view was that it is never quite as easy as one thinks, and once more reiterated, that while objective measures are "widely venerated" they are not that easy to develop, because one is faced with the difficulty of showing that what is being measured is actually the person's objective reality (1990a, p.45). Later, in his autobiography, Lazarus (1998) was to conclude that there were no real underlying problems between life events and daily hassles as measures of stress. Both, he suggested, were concerned with different but associated events in a person's life. Nevertheless, he was to go on and add, it was because of their proximal qualities that led him to favor a daily hassles approach, and it was this quality that made them, in his mind, a more useful tool for investigating the impact of typical stress on well-being.

The debate did produce some middle ground. Brown (1990), for example, argued that his *Life Events and Difficulties Schedule* (LEDS) "represents a position midway between that of Lazarus et al. (1985) and their critics Dohrenwend et al. (1984)" (pp. 19–22). The LEDS (Brown and Harris, 1986) involves semi-structured interviews in "order to obtain a full account of any reported event and its personal significance for the respondent" (Lipowski, 1986c, p.17). Each event is then rated using normative ratings capturing the "likely appraisal of a typical person rather then the actual appraisal of that particular individual" (Brown, 1990, p.20). The idea behind this approach is that the comprehensive collection of biographical and contextual material through a structured interview and the rating of this in a normative way "can go a long way to provide us with an 'objective' assessment of such appraisals" (Brown, 1990, p.20). In this way it recognizes, on the one hand, the importance of appraisal whilst meeting the competing view that events should not be 'contaminated' by the persons subjective response, on the other.

The importance of this approach, argues Brown (1990), lies in the way the interview data can be processed. The use of intense semistructured interviews "is likely to bring the kind of sensitivity, accuracy, and control of potential bias in reporting of life events that is required" (Brown, 1990, p.20). Lazarus (1990a) was to comment that he found the crux of Brown's views compatible with his own. On the use of interviews versus questionnaires to collect life event–hassles data, Lazarus (1990a), foreshadowing perhaps the debate that was yet to come, suggested that, essentially if researchers are going to come to terms with what may be good or not so good in terms of methodology, then when it comes to stress research both approaches are necessary. However, Lazarus (1990a) added, from his point of view, the use of in-depth, holistic-style approaches, well thought out, and planned are given less recognition than they deserve by stress researchers and so their potential as an explanatory tool is consistently being underplayed.

The debate about confounding and objective-subjective stressor measurement was something more than a debate about critical life events versus daily hassles and uplifts, although it was, to begin with, argued out in that context. It was much more fundamental than that, because it was a debate aimed at the very nature of stress, and those psychological processes that link the individual to the environment. It was a debate about theory, a new-look psychology (Lazarus, 1999), which saw a transition to cognitive mediation and a rebellion against methodological preciousness. It is a debate that occurs time and time again in the history of stress, because it has at its heart how we conceptualize stress, how we measure it and how we explain our results. It is for stress the never ending story because it reflects where we have been, where we are now, and where we are going. We will keep returning to it, just as we will return to the work of Lazarus and the pioneering and lasting contribution he made to the field of stress research.

But what happened to stressful life-events research? The enthusiasm for this sort of research has waned considerably. The reasons for this, Lazarus (1999) argued, lay partly in the failure to take into account individual meanings and coping and partly because the list of events did not keep up-to-date or comprehensive enough. Lists of events "do pose methodological problems, however, so students of stress outcomes are probably better advised to focus on a single fateful event, such as bereavement or technological disaster" (Costa and McCrae, 1990, p.23). Changing social and economic conditions may also have been responsible for researchers accepting that certain major events such as unemployment, for example, have widespread effects, and so singled them out for investigation rather than continuing with the more traditional approach of focusing on the accumulated effect of different stressful life events.

Personality and Type A Behavior Patterns

Continuing for a time in the footsteps of psychosomatic theory one of the core questions identified by this field of research asked "which personality variables increase susceptibility to, or resistance to illness." Stressful life events may be predictive of the onset of illness but to better understand the pathways through which this occurs "we still need to study personality variables and enduring behavior patterns as well as chronic life situations and social conditions for clues to etiology" (Lipowski, 1977a, p.240). The study of personality variables and behavior patterns must "help identify who is at risk, from what disease, and when" (Lipowski, 1977a, p.240).

We begin by exploring Type A behavior patterns. The idea of a "coronary-prone personality" (Friedman and Booth-Kewley, 1987, p.540) has a long history. Chesney and Rosenman (1980), for example, refer to the 1892 writings of the Canadian physician William Osler who described the coronary-prone individual as "a keen and ambitious man, [sic] the indicator of whose engines are set at full speed ahead" (see Chesney and Rosenman, 1980, p.188). It was in the 1950s that Friedman and Rosenman (1959), building on their earlier work "observed that their coronary heart disease patients shared a characteristic pattern of behaviors and emotional reactions they labeled as Type A behaviors" (Ganster, 1987, p.67). This behavior Friedman and Rosenman described as an "emotional complex" pattern, was primarily characterized by "intense ambition, competitive 'drive,' constant preoccupation with occupational 'deadlines,' and a sense of time urgency" (1959, p.1295). The absence of this behavior pattern was termed Type B. In reviewing their data Friedman and Rosenman indicated that it was significant that patients "with clinical coronary disease, many of them already have been found to exhibit many of the qualities making up the [Type A] behavior pattern" (1959, p.1294). Friedman and Rosenman were to conclude that whatever was responsible for this behavior pattern it was not confined to "any echelon of corporate or industrial life," that "it seemed to a ubiquitous and status-transcending phenomenon," and that it needed to be emphasized "that the stresses of this same society are of a variety never previously witnessed in any age of society" (1959, p.1294).

To investigate the relationship between coronary heart disease (CHD) and Type A behavior further, Rosenman with his colleague Friedman and others, followed 3500 males in an eight-and-a-half-year study known as the *Western Collaborative Group Study* (Rosenman, Friedman, Straus et al., 1964; Rosenman,

Brand, Jenkins, Friedman, Straus, and Wurm, 1975). The results of this prospective study "confirmed the behaviour pattern as a precursor of CHD, independent of the standard risk factors" (Chesney and Rosenman, 1980, p.189). Rosenman and his colleagues were to conclude that their findings "would appear to have important clinical implications for the primary prevention of CHD. Moreover, evaluating patients with CHD for presence of the coronary-prone behavior pattern may well improve the prognostic prediction of the course of the disease" (Rosenman et al., 1975, p.877).

For 40 years, the Type A behavior pattern has maintained a central position in research into personality and coronary heart disease. However, studies have challenged the role of Type A behavior in the development of coronary heart disease "with results varying considerably depending upon the method of measuring Type A behavior patterns" (Edwards, 1991, p.151). The two primary methods of assessing Type A behavior patterns are the Structured Interview (SI) and the Jenkins Activity Survey (JAS) (see Booth-Kewley and Friedman, 1987; Edwards, 1991). While, from these reviews, there was some cautious support for the SI as a tool for assessing Type A behavior patterns, a second finding from these reviews was to raise even more questions in the minds of researchers. The finding suggested that the traditional practice of measuring Type A by collapsing the constellation of behaviors into a single index should be abandoned in favor of measures that focus on the distinct behaviors themselves. "Separating existing global measures into their constituent components may reveal previously undetected relationships" (Edwards and Baglioni, 1991, p.287).

The evidence pointed in favor of this conclusion as well. "The hard-driving and competitive aspects of the Type A personality may be somewhat related to CHD but the speed and job-involvement aspects are probably not" (Booth-Kewley and Friedman, 1987, pp.357–8). Similarly the anger/hostility aspect of Type A behavior may be a more powerful predictor of risk than other Type A components (Cooper and Bright, 2001; Ganster, Schaubroeck, Sime, and Mayes, 1991), although the mechanisms through which anger and hostility might have an impact remain unclear. An approach that has gained some support among researchers (see Barling, Kelloway, and Cheung, 1996; Jex, 1998), has been to assess Type A behavior in terms of two components, "achievement strivings" (working harder) and "impatience-irritability" (showing annoyance with others). In this way "researchers have essentially captured the positive aspects of Type A in achievement strivings and the negative aspects in impatience-irritability" (Jex, 1998, p.80). The general feeling seems to be that by developing these separate component measures "using appropriate validation procedures and explicitly modelling their interactions and relationships, our understanding of the determinants, nature, and consequences of Type A behavior patterns will be considerable enhanced" (Edwards, 1991, p.173).

With "Type A behavior documented as a CHD risk factor, it was logical to examine the prevalence of Type A behavior in the occupational environment and to examine its relationship to correlates of occupational success and stress" (Chesney and Rosenman, 1980, p.191). The picture that was to emerge led to a number of cautious conclusions (Chesney and Rosenman, 1980; Ganster, 1987; Jex, 1998). While there was evidence that Type A's may impose demands on themselves and describe their jobs as having more responsibility and greater workloads, "there is no convincing evidence from the organizational studies that the objective job demands facing Type A's are really higher than B's" (Ganster 1987, p.73) nor, it seems, do Type A's generally "report more job dissatisfaction, anxiety or depression than do Type B's" (Chesney and Rosenman, 1980, p.195). However, in terms of how Type A's respond to work situations involving, for example stress, it would be possible to speculate, based on laboratory findings "that the Type A person may be more likely than the Type B person to respond physiologically to the challenges that are ubiquitous in our modern social and work environments. Thus Type A workers, alert to these challenges, may find themselves frequently engaging in specific Type A behaviors, such as hostile competitiveness, that are linked with arousal and risk of CHD" (Chesney and Rosenman, 1980, p.202). However, the evidence associating Type A behavior with stress still remains equivocal. One reason for this is that although the Type A behavior pattern may have health implication, it "is a complex constellation of cognitive, behavioral, and physiological responses" (Ganster, 1987, p.81) requiring more focused measurement practices (Edwards, 1991; Edwards and Baglioni, 1991). A second reason may be that more attention should be given to conceptualizing the role of Type A behavior in the stress process (Cooper and Payne, 1991).

In summary, the general consensus seems to be "that Type A is worth keeping and pursuing further but also that Type A should be regarded as only one part of the coronary-prone personality" (Booth-Kewley and Friedman, 1987, p.355). Booth-Kewley and Friedman go on to suggest that "Overall, the picture of the coronary-prone personality emerging from this review does not appear to be that of the workaholic, hurried, impatient individual, which is probably the image most frequently associated with coronary proneness. Rather the true picture seems to be one of a person with one or more negative emotions" (1987, p.358). The way forward it seems is for research to focus on identifying the relevant aspects of Type A behavior in conjunction with refining assessment and measurement practices. The message is clear "personality and disease should be vigorously investigated" (Friedman and Booth-Kewley, 1987, p.552).

Towards the Study of Individual Differences

Because of a research tradition that places considerable emphasis on understanding differences between people in their perception of, and reaction to stress, it is not surprising that the curiosity of researchers led them inevitably to turn their attention to exploring the role of a range of individual differences. The "question of individual differences in relation to the experience and effects of stress and in relation to coping is virtually a defining characteristic of the more psychological approaches. As a result, much research effort has been expended in exploring their nature and role, and in trying to establish the natural 'laws' which govern their behavior" (Cox and Ferguson, 1991, p.7). This research was to result in a plethora of individual differences being studied (Cooper and Bright, 2001). While these have included "genetic and biological differences, differences in skills or cognitive capabilities and differences in the goals and motivations which propel people into different kind of situations" (Bartlett, 1998, p.65) they are often classified according to Payne's (1988) three categories. These three categories are: genetic, acquired, and dispositional. While, as Payne (1988) makes clear, there are obviously complex influences amongst the three categories, he does identify a number of questions which in many ways sums up the different approaches that have been taken when individual differences have been researched.

These questions (Payne, 1988, p.210) identified such issues as, for example, "how do individual differences relate to the development of symptoms of psychological strain.... how do individual differences relate to perceptions of stress in the environment.... do they act as moderators of the stress-strain relationship," and "do they affect the way people cope with stress?" Individual differences have been hypothesized as influencing the stressor-strain relationship in one of three ways: either *directly* or by operating as a *mediator* or *moderator* of the relationship. A direct effect is where the individual difference variable directly impacts on the level of strain. When individual difference variables operate as moderators then, they "alter the strength or direction of the stress-strain relationship" (Cooper and Bright, 2001, p.114). In this case, it is possible to hypothesize for example, that the relationship between stressor and strain would be much stronger for those individuals displaying Type A behavior. That is Type A moderates the stressor-strain relationship. When individual differences operate as mediators then they become "responsible for the transmission of an effect" (Cox and Ferguson, 1991, p.12). In this case the individual difference variable operates as a pathway through which the stressor travels to affect the strain. As Cox and Ferguson point out, the mediating role of individual differences "offers some explanation of *how* external physical events take on psychological meaning" (1991, p.12). Examining individual differences as mediators provides researchers with a mechanism for understanding more about the role they play in the stress process. Moderator research using different individual differences tends to support them more in a predictor role (Cox and Ferguson, 1991).

The list of individual difference variables studies is long and, using Payne's (1988, p.209) classification, would include under the heading of *genetic* – gender, constitution, intelligence, reactivity. Under the heading of *acquired* would be social class, education and age, whilst *dispositional* variables would cover, for example, trait anxiety/neuroticism, Type A, locus of control, self-esteem, and extroversion–introversion. Despite the "common sense argument that people differ in their responses to stress researchers have only just begun to unravel the complexity of these relationships" (Cooper and Bright, 2001, p.130). There is now as much written (see Bartlett, 1988; Cooper and Bright, 2001; Cooper, Dewe, and O'Driscoll, 2001, Cox and Ferguson, 1991; Parkes, 1994) about, for example, *negative affectivity* (a disposition to focus negatively on issues, be introspective with a greater tendency to report more stress and dissatisfaction), *hardiness* (a hardy personality encompasses a number of resistance resources including commitment, perceived control over events, and a tendency to view demands in terms of challenges) and *locus of control* (an expectation of control over event – internal locus of control – versus the expectation that much is up to fate – external locus of control) as there has been about the hostility dimension of Type A behavior patterns. All reviewers of individual difference variables agree that there is much work still to be done both in terms of measurement strategies, identifying appropriate methodological approaches and developing frameworks that integrate individual differences into the stress process. One individual difference that has not yet been discussed is coping. "For most of its history, the study of coping and adaptation has rarely been divorced from the study of individual differences" (Suls, David, and Harvey, 1996, p.711). We follow this history when we turn our attention to the concept of coping.

A Return to the 1950s and 1960s and a Change in Focus

While the psychosomatic tradition continued to influence stress research by propagating "a holistic and biopsychosomatic approach" (Lipowski, 1986c, p.20) to illness, other forces were also stirring. The early years of the twentieth century saw the rise in popularity of *behaviorism*. Although "its initial reception within psychology was cool or even grudging" (Viney, 1993, p.289), it was to have a profound influence on psychological thought and practice and very quickly came to dominate. Behaviorism in its most radical form claimed, "all forms of behavior are to be found outside the organism and therefore explanations of behavior in terms of physiological or mental events should be avoided" (Viney, 1993, p.368). However, the 1950s and 1960s saw a growing consensus that the vision offered by behaviorists "was too narrow, and that methodologically and substantively, they had closed too many doors" (Viney, 1993, p.345). A new broader approach to understanding behavior was called for and "one of the most conspicuous trends in psychology in the 1950s has been the renewed interest in cognition" (Viney, 1993, p.439).

The transition was not without controversy, fierce debate, or the taking of sides that demanded intense loyalty. The influence of behaviorism did not, of course, just disappear, nor did the "dogma of positivism" (Lazarus, 1999), to which it so rigidly subscribed. Psychologists were, however, interested in a "new-look psychology" that would open the door to the study of the mind by offering a wide variety of phenomena for investigation that simply were just not seen as necessary by radical behavior-ism (Lazarus, 1999, p.7). But even during the period of radical behaviorism the beliefs of cognitive psychology were always present and "did not disappear far from it" (Hergenhahn, 1992, p.542), but for many psychologists what they now wanted was a discipline that emphasized cognitive experience and a context that would allow that emphasis to flourish.

By the 1960s and 1970s, the stimulus–response (S–R) model of psychology, which was the heir of behaviorism, was slowly being put to one side (Lazarus, 1999). Described as "reduction-ist" (Aldwin, 2000), and conveying a "rather pinched outlook" (Lazarus 1999), the S–R model was transformed into a much more forward-looking *stimulus–organism–response (S–O–R) model* (Lazarus, 1999, p.7). Now the S–O–R model freed researchers to explore, with renewed enthusiasm, the nature of those mental processes that might be found in the "black box" of the mind and that helped to explain the way people behave (Lazarus, 1999). As Lazarus (1991) makes clear while the "O" stands for organism, it more commonly came to refer to those thoughts that mediate between the environment and the behavioral response, and it was these thoughts that became identified as having a causal influence. The inclusion of some sort of *cognitive mediation* (Lazarus, 1991; 1999) process in psychological models led many to see this period as some sort of cognitive revolution, but given the long history of cognitive psychology, as Lazarus (1999) ex-plained, the only time it could really be described as a revolution was when it was placed hard up against the views of radical behaviorism.

The S–R and the S–O–R models represented two forces or intellectual traditions in psychology; the outer-objective (exogenic) and the inner-subjective (endogenic). Psychology has always had a strong exogenic character "committed as it has been to rendering an account of objective knowledge of the world" (Gergen, 1985, p.269). This approach is illustrated by research on critical life events and the view that life events are external occurrences uncontaminated by personal meanings. Yet the 1960s and 1970s saw a "full force" return to the "endogenic perspective in the guise of cognitive psychology," where behavior is critically dependent on the "cognitive processing of information, that is, on the world as cognized rather than the world as is" (Gergen, 1985, p.269). Crucial aspects of knowledge are lost if the objective is emphasized at the expense of the subjective, and the challenge "has been to transcend the traditional object-subject dualism and all its attendant problems and to develop a new framework of analysis" (Gergen, 1985, p.270). If we carry this reasoning into the domain of stress research then, as Lazarus (1991) suggests, since *both* person (subjective) and environment (objective) are key players in stress and coping, the swing between one and the other could simply be ended as soon as researchers accept the relational nature of each to the other, and that both are part of the same transaction. All we need, Lazarus (1991) adds, is to find a suitable language that lets us describe the nature of this relational-transactional approach. The idea of applying a cognitive-relational framework to stress research was to have a profound impact on the field.

The shift in the 1950s and 1960s to a relational framework for investigating stress had "enormous implications, not only for the manner in which science is conducted, but for much of everyday life" (Aldwin, 2000, p.6). The work that flowed from this period was as pioneering and inspiring as the work of those from earlier decades. Paradigm changes send ripples in all sorts of directions, and the decades of stress research that were to follow are as much a debate about methods and approaches as they about advancing our understanding of stress. Never far from the center of any debate on stress are questions asking where are current methodologies taking us, and what can alternative methodologies offer? The question, as Lazarus (1990a) puts it, is whether we have become "too smug" (p.47) in our acceptance and use of traditional methods and procedures to even begin to think about, or look at, whether they are providing relevant answers to the questions we are asking, and whether the answers we are coming up with are as good as we can get. The debate surrounding methods is deeply engrained and pervades the whole history of stress – a part of its history that we will be returning to time and time again.

The History of Stress in Sweden

The foundation for stress research in Sweden was laid in the 1960s by Ulf von Euler, Professor of Physiology at the Karolinska Institute in Stockholm. Professor von Euler had developed methods for the measurement of the stress hormones adrenaline and noradrenaline in the urine. He was later to be awarded the Nobel Prize in Physiology and Medicine (1970) for this work. The development of such new methods were to become a key factor in future research programs aimed at studying the experience of stress in different situations, including work situations. Early stress research in Sweden focused on hospitalized patients, or was laboratory based using healthy subjects. It was now possible, building on the earlier work of Professor von Euler for research-ers to measure stress hormones levels using measures that could be taken outside the laboratory. Researchers were now able to follow people going about their everyday routines and still take exact measures of stress hormone levels (Frankenhaeuser, 1993).

Several researchers were inspired by the work of von Euler. One of the most well known was Professor Lennart Levi. In 1959, he founded the now-famous Stress Research Laboratory at Karolinska Institute, which was designated a WHO collaborating center for research and training in psychosocial factors and health. As a result of Levi's and his coworkers' research on the significance of the relationship between psychosocial factors and health, the National Institute for Psychosocial Factors and Health was founded in 1980, with Levi as its Director (Theorell, 1997). The influence of the work carried out at the Stress Research Laboratory was soon to be reflected in the Swedish work envir-onment law (SOU, 1976, p.1), particularly in relation to piece-work and night shiftwork.

A selection of Lennart Levi's most well-known publications can be found in "Four Decades of Lennart Levi's Research – A Selection," published (in English) by the Department of Stress Research, Karolinska Institute and the National Institute for

Psychosocial Factors and Health in celebration of his 60th birthday in 1990 (Levi, 1990). Papers in this collection range from early studies on fundamental aspects of stress to studies on piecework and nightwork and research on unemployment and population health (Theorell, 1997).

Issues relating to work-related stress and its impact on individual health and well-being had been discussed in Sweden for many decades. Bertil Gardell, Professor of Work Psychology at Stockholm University, was the first researcher to make associations between control/decision latitude at work and stress and psychosocial work problems (Gardell, 1971). These ideas inspired other researchers (Frese, 1977; Karasek, 1979; Karasek and Theorell, 1990). It is interesting to note that Robert Karasek (of University of Southern California) did some of his work leading to the formulation of the demand-control model at the Stress Research Laboratory of the Karolinska Institute in Stockholm in close cooperation mainly with Töres Theorell. Further work in Sweden saw the Karasek model expanded to include social support (Johnson, 1986). The demand–control model was to inspire stress research across the world. However the model is not without controversy with research yielding conflicting results.

Marianne Frankenhaeuser, Professor of Psychology at the Karolinska Institute and a colleague of Levi, was instrumental in including theories and methods from psychophysiological stress research into traditional working life research. One of her many thesis was that our biological "equipment" had undergone a much slower development than technology and society. This ever-increasing discrepancy puts high demands on our ability to adjust (Frankenhaeuser, 1981; Frankenhaeuser and Ödman, 1983). Her research aimed at understanding the causes of stress, defining contributing work and organizational factors and identifying factors protecting people from harmful stress. The results can then be used as a basis for prevention and intervention (Frankenhaeuser and Johansson, 1986). Another important aspect of Frankenhaeuser's research were the studies on gender related differences in stress levels and stress perception (Frankenhaeuser, 1991; 1993; Lundberg, Mårdberg and Frankenhaeuser, 1994). One of the most striking differences between men and women that are shown in this research is the ability to relax when coming home from work. At about five o'clock in the afternoon, stress hormones and blood pressure go down in men while they go up in the women. This is particularly true for female professionals.

In a recent contribution to a textbook on stress Levi (2002) concluded that although researchers today study stress reactions and their causes multifactorially they presuppose a linear relationship. Levi advocates a nonlinear, interactionistic, and systems analytic approach at several levels from molecular to organizational to societal. Another important direction for future stress research has been discussed by Arnetz (2002) who emphasized the importance of addressing work-related stress at the organizational level, the critical role of management to address such stress and the ability of management to optimize the competitiveness of the organization by also considering biological aspects of work.

The Origins of Organizational Psychology

The 1950s and 1960s saw other developments that were also to enrich the history of stress. One of these was the growth and maturity of organizational psychology, and the application of psychological techniques and methods to work settings. Work stress research was to generate volumes of research, and create an enthusiasm for stress that has continued unabated to the present day. Not without its own controversies and debates, occupational psychology has a history spanning much of the twentieth century. The nature and scope of organizational psychology was profoundly influenced by two World Wars, where demands for increased productivity brought with it a need to understand how factors like fatigue, for example, affected the health and efficiency of workers. "Even the enlightened few who were aware of what psychology had to offer on the industrial front could not of foreseen its pervasive impact on the conduct of war" (Shimmin and Wallis, 1994, p.18). The tremendous contribution psychologists made in terms of selection and assessment during the war years, coupled with the work on leadership, added new depth to the growing field of industrial psychology, with the discipline that we now know as organizational or occupational psychology beginning to take shape.

Other initiatives were also nudging the emerging field of industrial psychology towards a focus on work stress. One of these was the launch, in the late 1950s, of a program of research to understand the impact of the organization on the individual at The University of Michigan, as a joint effort by the Survey Research Center and the Research Center for Group Dynamics. The research aims of this program was "concerned with developing research methods, theory, and substantive findings which treat fully the influences of the contemporary environment on mental health" (Kahn, Wolfe, Quinn, Snoek, and Rosenthal, 1964, p.vii). The focus of much of this work was on "the mental health of the adult, with special attention to social psychological factors in large scale organizations" (French and Kahn, 1962, p.1). A review of the work carried out by this program in 1962 concluded that "the findings may best be viewed as evidence that social psychological research on the origins and consequences of behavior relevant to mental health is under way and that future research can confidently be expected to expand upon and integrate results such as those described" (Zander and Quinn, 1962, p.63).

In Britain "interest on the part of government officials and industrialists in this topic [occupational stress] was aroused in the late 1960s by high levels of sickness absence among industrial workers. These levels appeared to be associated with symptoms of illness and psychological disorder thought to be 'stress-related'" (Shimmin and Wallis, 1994, p.98). Accordingly, "a programme of research into occupational stress was initiated by the Medical Research Council, supported by the Department of Employment and the Trade Union Congress" (Shimmin and Wallis, 1994, p.98). Even at this early stage, there were concerns as to whether adequate field research would prove possible or would make a difference to work practices but "research into stress soon got under way at a number of locations and the late seventies saw the flowering of many studies by occupational psychologists and other specialists, directed at all manner of jobs and occupations" (Shimmin and Wallis, 1994, p.99).

There was, in Britain, as in the United States, a strong social emphasis in examining work behavior, and the work of the Tavistock Institute in the late 1940s early 1950s into the behavior of groups in work settings captured the "imagination of social scientists from a number of disciplines concerned with social and technological changes in the workplace" (Shimmin and Wallis, 1994, p.87). This early work of the Tavistock Institute provided one of the most "enduring multi-level frameworks for considering individuals, groups and organizations in relation to their environments (Shimmin and Wallis, 1994, p.87). Interestingly, the Survey Research Center at the University of Michigan and the Tavistock Institute in Britain, because of their similar aims based around a "focus on human relations within organizations" (Newton, 1995, p.32), maintained close links with each other, with both providing instructive directions for research into health and well-being in the workplace. So began, in both countries, what French and Kahn referred to as a "programmatic approach to studying the industrial environment and mental health" (1962, p.1).

The Rise of Ergonomic/Human Factors

The World Wars were also the catalyst that saw the "initial rise of interest in the relationship between man [*sic*] and the working environment" (Oborne, 1987, p.4) and then the transformation of this interest into the field of ergonomics or human factors. July 1949 is pinpointed as the time, when in Britain, "an interdisciplinary group was formed (the Human Research Group) for those interested in human work problems and by February 1950 the term *ergonomics* was adopted and the discipline could finally be said to be born" (Oborne, 1987, p.4). Ergonomics arose out of a need to consider how individuals cope with their environment and reflects a multidisciplinary field of study where a range of disciplines come together "to maximize safety, efficiency and comfort by shaping the 'machine' to the operator's capabilities" (Oborne, 1987, p.6). A similar history can be found in the United States, where following the Second World War, the Department of Defense continued to recognize the value of what was then called *human engineering* or *engineering psychology* (Howell, 1991, p.211). By the late 1950s, after some trouble agreeing on a name, the discipline emerged as *human factors*, with a focus on what was then, and what still remains today as its analytic cornerstone the "attempt to improve the fit between humans and technology. What has changed is our understanding of human performance and the factors that control it" (Howell, 1991, p.212). What has not changed is that "psychology is still the best (though certainly not the only) source of theories on human performance" (Howell, 1991, p.212).

This discipline has made a substantial contribution to our understanding of stress. Not surprisingly, there are clear similarities between an engineering model of stress and the approach adopted by ergonomics-human factors. In general, most ergonomists approach stress by first suggesting that there are optimal conditions for performance and reasonable levels of work intensity. It is when performance is required under environmental conditions that depart from, or are outside of reasonable limits that some form of stress is imposed. Returning to the engineering analogy, individuals, like physical systems, may be able to tolerate certain levels of stress "but when it becomes intolerable permanent damage, physiological and psychological, may result" (Cox, 1978, p.13). Stress, from this point of view, is frequently discussed in terms of the relationship between levels of performance and concepts such as arousal, signal detection theory, and different environmental demands. While the underlying theme from this work emphasizes that it is those situations that tax individual capabilities that cause stress, there is also the recognition that the "interaction between an operator and the environment is a very complex event" and "it is now important to question how this complexity can interfere with work performance" (Oborne, 1987, pp.8-9). A hint perhaps, that to try and understand this complexity requires researchers to consider those psychological processes that link the individual and the environment.

Summary

The 1950s and 1960s provided fertile ground for stress researchers. Change was in the wind, and there was a real sense of urgency as researchers strove to take advantage of new opportunities, new ideas, and new frameworks for doing research. Different developments each have their own history and at the same time contribute to the sum that makes up a history of stress. At times researchers appear to accept the need for change at the conceptual level, but continue to research, unaware or unable to accept, that established practices and methods might need to be rethought. The greatest danger that emerged from this period and one, which continues to haunt stress research "lies not in the abundance of ideas and creative opportunities but that many researchers will simply nod wisely but continue with their own work believing that such opportunities are best left to others" (Dewe, 2001, p.92). The 1950s and 1960s provided the opportunity for a period of quiet reconstruction in stress research. Whether this time, and the opportunities that were available, were exploited to the full by researchers can be judged by what unfolds in the following pages.

CHAPTER FOUR

The Work of Richard Lazarus

Introduction

Richard Lazarus is "arguably the most influential scholar in this area in the twentieth century" (Daniels, 2001, p.802). His work has been described as "influential" (Horowitz, 1990, p.25), as making "a pioneering and lasting contribution" (Ben-Porath and Tellegen, 1990, p.14), and leaving researchers "fascinated by his programmatic demand to radically change the outlook, research paradigm, and conceptual language of stress research" (Weber and Laux, 1990, p.37). Lazarus in his own quiet and unassuming way is more modest, stating that after 50 years of stress research, "I would like to believe I have thrown some useful light on the never-ending effort to understand" (Lazarus, 1998a, p.404).

Research scholars are, as Lazarus (1993) suggests, products of their times. Not only are they influenced by the outlook of their generation but their work changes the outlook for those that follow. This means that to understand one you must also understand the other. This ebb and flow of ideas provides a context for understanding "why we are where we are," and operates as a means of determining what is significant and what is not. This is as true for the study of stress, as it is for the study of any concept. One of the most profound influences in stress research following the Second World War was the work of Richard Lazarus. In the next part of our history we explore the enormous contribution Richard Lazarus has made in pursuing his ideas about stress, by describing those events that capture the richness of his work from post Second World War to the present – a period of 50 years of stress research.

The Beginnings

Lazarus (1993) describes, how when he first appeared on the scene, psychology and psychologists showed only a modicum of interest in "stress," seeing it as something other than a mainstream concept, and giving little, if any, thought to its application to everyday life. It was his work for the military that began, what was to become a lifetime devoted to unraveling the stress process. From this work, he and his colleagues quickly discovered that how one person reacted to stressful conditions did not necessarily mean that others would react in the same way. Their conclusion was that to understand what was happening you had to take account of *"individual differences in motivational and cognitive* variables which intervened between the stressor and the reaction" (Lazarus, 1993, p.3). At the time of this hypothesis, Lazarus (1993) was to recall that psychology had hardly begun to move from stimulus-response (S-R) models, and so, there was an uneasiness about individual differences, with the scientific dogma of the time, arguing "that the role of science was to develop general laws" (p.3) and that when there appeared to be variations from these laws, the immediate response, in line with the thinking of the day, was to simply explain them in terms of measurement error.

The blossoming of the cognitive movement in the 1960s and the intellectual transition towards stimulus — organism–response (S–O–R) models was encouraged by a new-look psychology. The research that emerged from this "new-look" movement offered a view of perception that showed that individual attitudes, beliefs, expectations, and motives influence perceptions of the environment (Lazarus, 1998a). It was the work of this movement, and those earlier writers who, in the face of radical behaviorism, were prepared to suggest, and stand by, a much more subjective view of human behavior - looking to individual differences in goals and values as a source of variation in behavior (Lazarus, 1998a), that heavily influenced Lazarus's work (1993). The seeds that were to grow into the belief that cognitive mediation is at the heart of psychological stress (Lazarus, 1993), were sown and the concepts of appraising and appraisals that define this mediating process began to take root.

The work of Lazarus and his colleagues in the 1960s also helped to change the minds of many who were stilled attached to an S-R formulation that appraisals are fundamental to stress responses (see Lazarus, 1993) What began as a "powerful tide" eventually became a "tidal wave that seems to have swept old epistemologies aside," moving psychology from behaviorism to an outlook where psychologists began to abandon any hesitancy that they may previously have had about using mental processes to explain individual actions and reaction (Lazarus, 1993, p.6). The scene was now set where psychologists could begin to explore, in a much more systematic way, how individual reactions were influenced by what was going on in the mind (Lazarus, 1993).

The Berkeley Stress and Coping Project

Lazarus (1998) talks about the Berkeley Stress and Coping Project as passing through three incarnations. The first covered the period soon after Lazarus arrived at Berkeley in 1957 and at this time was devoted to the pursuit of film studies and his early work on the *influence of appraisal*. The second incarnation in the 1960s reflected an increased interest in *emotions and coping*, whereas the third began the transition from laboratory to field research. It was in this third incarnation beginning around 1977 that Lazarus (1998) wanted to explore how, without giving up his commitment to a theoretical position that emphasized appraisals and coping, it could be applied to everyday life. Lazarus (1998) wanted his research to be change or process oriented, which is what he argued stress is mainly about, because, as he noted, being under stress is all about wanting to change the stressful encounter.

However, as Lazarus (1998) was to acknowledge, thinking it is important and desirable to investigate the causes of stress in people's lives and how they cope is one thing, developing an "adequate blueprint" (p.191) as to how to go about it is another – so when it came to the specifics he was, as he noted, somewhat vague. However, a study by Cohen and Lazarus in 1973, which showed that, when compared with a dispositional coping measure, measuring coping as a process was a more effective predictor of both coping and outcomes made Lazarus (1998) all the more convinced he was heading in the right direction and it was time, by the late 1970s, to put the laboratory behind him and focus on stress and coping as they happen in everyday life. So the foundations for the third incarnation of the *Berkeley Stress and Coping Project* were in place, and it was this phase of the project, even more than the phases that preceded it, which was to be extremely productive and influential.

It was in this third incarnation that Lazarus (1998) presented the case for his theory of stress by focusing on two main concepts, *appraisal* and *coping*. For this work Lazarus and his colleagues developed in the early 1980s the *Hassles and Uplifts Scale* and the *Ways of Coping Interview-Questionnaire*. The development of these two instruments and the work that followed from their use had an immediate, fundamental and lasting effect on stress research. The significance of the work using the *Hassles and Uplifts Scale*, and the debate it generated we have described. Working on the *Ways of Coping Questionnaire* with his colleague Susan Folkman produced work that has become some of the most cited work in the field (e.g. Lazarus and Folkman, 1984), both in the United States and abroad. The coping questionnaire was to become the most widely used questionnaire in research on coping and produced replicable findings about how the coping process worked (Lazarus, 1998). The history of coping research is still ahead of us.

It was during this third incarnation that also saw a shift in emphasis by Lazarus from psychological stress to emotions. Beginning in the 1960s Lazarus (see 1998), became increasingly troubled with the practice of treating stress as a unidimensional variable where people simply placed themselves on a scale that measured, at one end a little stress and at the other considerable stress. To Lazarus (1998) this was a rather restrictive and somewhat bland way of measuring reactions, when compared to the wide variety of emotions that stress actually produced. Every emotion, Lazarus (1998) argued, had a very different story to tell about the importance of what is happening to a person and it is "this large panoply of emotions that conveys the richness and complexity of the human mind and the continuing struggle to adapt" (Lazarus, 1998, p.209). It was just a short step from here to the idea of *core relational meanings* (Lazarus, 1991; 1999), where each emotion involves a different appraisal pattern, and a pathway for exploring the appraisal, coping, and emotion relationship was established.

The idea of relational meanings and their association with appraisals was to produce considerable, and at times intense, debate. The powerful nature of this idea is captured, when Lazarus (1998a) described the transaction between the person and the environment as being defined in terms of individual meanings. It is these meanings, Lazarus (1998a) added, that are the prime source of emotions and coping. The Berkeley Project came to an end in 1988. By that time the project had given the field a view on stress that was process oriented and transactional, encompassing appraisals, coping, and emotions. The work of Lazarus and his many colleagues in the Berkeley Project caught the imagination of supporter and critic alike. Fifteen years on from the end of the Berkeley Project, their work is still being discussed, debated, and examined. The work produced by Lazarus and his group of researchers is still at the center of stress research. The hope that Lazarus expressed "that interest in, and effective research on the coping process and human adaptation continues with vigor and dedication" (Lazarus, 1998, p.210) has been realized.

A Historical Look at Appraisal

Psychological stress, as Lazarus suggests in his 1966 book, refers to a particular kind of relationship between the person and the environment. It is one in which the demands of any encounter tax or exceed the person's resources. The "unit of analysis" in this transaction is appraisal. It is this appraisal process that links the person and the environment. Once a transaction has been appraised as "stressful" coping processes are initiated to "manage the troubled person-environment relationship and these processes influence the person's subsequent appraisal and hence the kind and intensity of the stress reaction. This cognitive-relational view, which once had to overcome entrenched behavioristic resistance, is now all but dominant" (Lazarus, 1990, p.1). While, as Lazarus (1990) suggested, concepts like appraisal and coping are part of a stress researchers routine vocabulary exploring their historical development is still instructive.

Lazarus (1966; 1993; 1998a; 1999; 2001) provides a number of sources for reviewing, historically, the concept of appraisal. Talking about the central role that appraisal plays in his theory of psychological stress, Lazarus (1998a), in his book *Fifty Years of the Research and Theory of R.S. Lazarus: An Analysis of Historical and Perennial Issues* commented, that as his work spanned the years from the early 1960s onwards he had some difficulty remembering when exactly it was, that he first began using the term appraisal. So, in preparation for writing this book, he went back through his early work of the 1950s and 1960s to trace when the term first appeared. Even though, as Lazarus discovered, he first used the term in 1964, and the concept in a systematic theoretical way from 1966 there is a rich history in how the concept evolved. It was Lazarus's interest in individual differences in stress that led him to see these individual differences in terms of the personal significance a person gives to what is happening. Greatly impressed by the work of Grinker and Spiegel (1945), and armed with the belief that stress had to do with personal meanings, Lazarus as he explained in his book reviewing his work (1998a) soon began to explain individual differences in stress responses in terms of, for example, "personal meanings", or the "subjects definition of the situation" (1998a, p.392). Personal meanings require an evaluation in essence an appraisal. This idea as Lazarus was to note later, was in his work right from the very beginning and was to become the "hallmark" of his approach (Lazarus, 1998a).

For a time Lazarus used the term perception rather than appraisal. His shift to using the term appraisal, he credits to the pioneering work of Arnold (1960). Perception, Lazarus (1998a) recalled when reviewing the discussions of the 1960s, seemed to him, to be too narrow a term for what he had in mind, because it didn't really capture the true essence of appraisal, as some sort of judgment about the significance of an encounter, even though, in the way he was using the word, he meant it to carry this notion. Spurred on by Arnold's cognitive-mediational approach that seemed to Lazarus to be entirely relevant to psychological stress, appraisal became, "for good reason," (1999, p.74) the operative word, since appraisal much more than perception reinforces the notion of some sort of evaluation of what was going on. It was also around this time as Lazarus notes in 2001 that he began his theorizing about appraisal in his theory of stress. There are two kinds of appraising: primary and secondary and although they are interdependent they are discussed separately.

The process of evaluating the significance of a transaction between the person and the environment in terms of well-being is described as *primary appraisal*. The fundamental question in primary appraisal is "whether anything is at stake?" If, the appraisal that is made is that that the encounter is stressful then the transactional alternatives are harm/loss [damage already occurred], threat [possibility of damage in the future] or challenge [an opportunity for growth, mastery or gain]" (Lazarus, 1999, p.76). Later, as Lazarus was to shift his focus from stress to emotions, he identified another kind of appraisal which he called "benefit." This appraisal was introduced because, as Lazarus noted in 2001, some account needed to be taken of positive emotions and for them there needed to be a different route linking them to patterns of appraisal. There is also the question of whether appraisals like for example, "threat" and "challenge" can occur in the same transaction. The answer Lazarus (2001) gives is that they may although one or the other usually dominates. As the process of appraising unfolds, what was once a threat can be converted into a challenge and vice versa.

Secondary appraisal refers to the process that focuses on "what can be done" about a stressful transaction. This appraisal is concerned with evaluating coping options. It is not coping as such but it is the cognitive underpinnings for coping (Lazarus, 1999). In any stressful transaction, argues Lazarus (2001), we must evaluate the available coping options and on that basis decide what to do. There had, as Lazarus recalled in his 1999 book, some ambiguity and difficulty as to what to call this phase of the appraisal process, as it is often very difficult to actually separate appraisals and coping. This issue is made even more complex, as Lazarus was to continue to point out, as appraisals and coping go "hand in hand" and this simply contributes to the uncertainty, as to whether in any encounter, what is being thought or done is appraisal or coping or both. Also, the use of the term "secondary" is not meant to suggest a process of any less importance, as one type of appraisal never operates independently of the other. So, Lazarus (1999) noted, if they are to be discussed separately then what needs to be remembered is that the distinguishing feature is not one of timing but one of content.

The issues raised by the complexity and process oriented focus of the appraisal process, and the question of "what process is occurring," must always be built on an in-depth understanding of what the person is thinking and doing in any encounter (Lazarus, 1999). So, the fundamental importance of appraisals and their role in the stress process cannot, as we shall see, be separated from a debate about methodology. More importantly, it is a debate about whether researchers are "bold enough" to confront the fact that traditional methods may no longer be capable of providing the understanding that is required (Lazarus, 1999).

The Nature of Appraisals and the Debate that Followed

It was in a 1995 article that Lazarus identified a number of "vexing research problems inherent in cognitive-mediational theories of emotions" (p.183). One of these concerned the *nature* of appraisals, and whether the appraisal process is *conscious or unconscious*. Early in his work Lazarus described his treatment of appraising as being conscious and deliberate. Lazarus (1999) noted, in this respect, that it was probably unnecessary to continually use, in relation to appraisals, the cognitive prefix. It was used initially to focus attention on the complexity of the evaluative processes involved. As Lazarus shifted his attention from stress to emotions, so began a process that led him to review the nature of appraising. Lazarus was taken by the ideas of Arnold (1960) who viewed appraising as instantaneous rather than deliberate. Originally, wrote Lazarus "I thought that Arnold had underemphasized the complexity of evaluative judgments . . . and I still do. . . . [Now,] I am more impressed with the instantaneity of the process of appraising even in complex and abstract instances" (Lazarus, 2001, p.51).

Since his original work (1966) there has been, as Lazarus notes, a remarkable attitude change taking place in psychology, with researchers becoming interested in unconscious processing. By the 1980s and 1990s this interest had exploded into questions as to 'what was unconscious,' 'what did this mean,' and in relation to the field of stress "whether an appraisal can be unconscious" (Lazarus, 1995; 1999; 2001). In relation to the last question

Lazarus answers with a resounding "yes." However, this sudden surge of interest, and research, did Lazarus (1999) suggest, tend to focus on what could be described as the cognitive unconscious.

Cognitive unconscious (see Lazarus, 1991a; 1995; 1990; 2001) is an unconsciousness that results from inattention. It comes about for a number of reasons but the important emphasis here, Lazarus (1995) suggests, is on the idea of "automatizing" what has already received attention. So, Lazarus (1999) suggests, there are two main contrasting ways an appraisal may come about. The first can be "deliberate and largely conscious," where as the second may be "intuitive, automatic and unconscious" (Lazarus, 1999, p.82). Both, Lazarus (1999) emphasizes, require some cognitive activity. The reluctance to accept the latter point of view may, as Lazarus (1990a) suggests, have less to do with the explanatory potential of the notion of appraisal and more to do with the fact that unconscious appraisal raise some fairly fundamental methodological issues about how such appraisals are recognized and measured. These distinctions are not made any easier if, as Lazarus (1995) suggests, appraisals that were at one time deliberate can, over time become more automated a sort of short-circuiting where the same appraisal is made automatically without much attention being paid to what is going on. This idea that, deliberate appraisals can, over time, be automated, raises, as Lazarus suggests, questions about whether we need to know more about how these different types of appraisals work before it is possible to accept as valid that deliberate appraisals are more likely to be conscious and automatic appraisal more likely to be unconscious (Lazarus, 1995).

These sorts of issues, acknowledged by Lazarus as difficulties when confronting conscious and unconscious appraisals, are just part of a wider debate about the role of appraisals in the stress process that continues to be argued out. The most well-known of these arguments was the debate beginning in the 1980s between Lazarus and Zajonc around the issue of whether emotions require cognition, or more accurately, whether affect, defined more broadly to embrace a range of experiences including emotions, require cognition? The *American Psychologist* was the main 'venue' for the discussion that took place. Zajonc's (1980; 1984) argument was that "affective judgments may be fairly independent of, and precede in time, the sorts of perceptual and cognitive operations commonly assumed to be the basis of these affective judgments" (1980, p.151). Zajonc went on to argue, "that for most decisions, it is extremely difficult to demonstrate that there has actually been *any* prior cognitive process whatsoever" (1980, p.155). In 1984, Zajonc was to restate his argument that although affect and cognition "ordinarily function conjointly, affect could be generated without, a prior cognitive process" (1984, p.117).

Lazarus (1991b) described the debate that followed as "remarkable" because of its "verve, thoughtfulness, [and] diversity" adding "Zajonc had touched a nerve and uncovered an unresolved set of modern issues that apparently had lain dormant in the minds of many psychologists" (p.7). Lazarus (1982) in his rebuttal restated his long held position that cognitive appraisal is about the meanings and significance one gives to any encounter and therefore is fundamental to the type of emotional response. The question, argued Zajonc (1984), of whether affect can occur independently must be settled on empirical grounds. How can we be sure, argued Zajonc, that some process of appraisal has taken place? What type of evidence would be required, countered Lazarus (1984), to show that emotions and cognitions are independent or that emotions can precede cognitive activity. While, suggests Lazarus, "the scales of plausibility might be tipped in favor of affective primacy" (1984, p.126) Zajonc can "no more prove that a cognition is *not* present ... than I can prove it *is* present" (1984, p.126). "I doubt," Lazarus was to write, "that the debate can be resolved by research data. Therefore, we are forced to rely largely on logic and theory, while keeping an eye out for observations that could help us evaluate the tenability of our assumptions, propositions and hypotheses" (1991b, p.16)

Following Zajonc's original article, the Lazarus-Zajonc debate ebbed and flowed over six years with a number of other commentators adding to the discussion. But it was not the only issue being debated. The objective versus subjective measurement of stress continued to divide researchers. The idea of events being appraised in terms of personal meanings still left many researchers uneasy and arguing that "it is perfectly reasonable to analyze the objective environmental events, because some events may be presumed to be stressful for most individuals" (Costa and McCrae, 1990, p.23). While the measurement of a truly objective event may be somewhat of a challenge proponents of this side of the argument based their belief that it could be done, using the rational, that it must be entirely possible to identify events that can be assumed to be stressful to all. Whether such an approach is truly objective is a moot point argues Lazarus (1990), because they too must carry an element of "subjective consensus," and so what may be significant to one person may not to another. Even critical life events, Lazarus (1990) argued, do not always produce the same coping activities or emotional responses. What those who argue for objective measurement must do, Lazarus (1990) concluded, is to show how the objective measures they are using tell us as much about the stress process as subjective measurement do. The debate continues.

The publication of his book in the late 1990s (1999) gave Lazarus an opportunity to deal with a critique of appraisal theory outlined by Parkinson and Manstead (1992). "We only take issue with Lazarus on the question of whether cognitive appraisal is the *only* route to the apprehension of the personal meaning of objects, events, or relationships" (Parkinson and Manstead, 1992, p.139). The thrust of their argument is that while appraisals are intimately involved in the process "they are never the exclusive determinant of emotion" (Parkinson and Manstead, 1992, p.123). While the difficulties of accessing and measuring appraisals are not lost on these authors, from their perspective, "the grammar of emotion is distributed through social as well as cognitive networks" (1992, p.146). Parkinson, in a later article, was to reaffirm the view that "appraisal representations are often steps along the way to emotion" (2001, p.180), but are not a complete explanation, going on to suggest "the whole story can only emerge when the route linking these steps and connecting them to emotional outcomes is mapped out more thoroughly" (2001, p.180). Lazarus, in response, turned his argument on the basis that the only substantive disagreement between them "is whether appraisal is a *necessary factor* rather than merely a sufficient factor in the emotion process" (1999, p.97). Acknowledging the methodological difficulties outlined by Parkinson and Manstead, and the challenges that all researchers face when exploring the appraisal process, Lazarus (1999) concluded, that despite the evidence presented by Parkinson and Manstead, the empirical case is not yet strong enough for him to give up his long-held meaning-centered approach, where cognitive mediation is the principal factor in emotion arousal.

The explanatory potential of the concept of appraisal, fundamental to Lazarus's transactional mediational theory of stress, is
not in doubt. Understandably the debate has focused on process,
and those elements that make up that process. Most commentators would agree that researching such processes requires a
rethink in terms of the appropriateness of traditional methodologies if we are to better understand the arguments being made
about the nature of appraisals, the appraising process and its
impact on emotions. Lazarus (1990) summed up what might be
involved by emphasizing how critical *meaning* is to emotions, but
suggesting at the same time that other ways need to be found to
uncover these meanings other than through inferring it from
what a person tells us. In a glimpse of what may be the way
forward for stress research Lazarus (1990) comments that more
and more convincing reasons are emerging to believe that "longitudinal, in-depth, and holistic-styled research" (p.47) will
provide richer and more enlightening information about what
an individual is thinking, feeling, and doing than continuing to
rely on well-worn, traditional data collection methods.

Lazarus and the Process View of Coping

"In my view," Lazarus argues, "stress itself as a concept pales in
significance for adaptation compared with coping" (1998a,
p.202). To understand the dynamics of stress, argues Lazarus
(1998), researchers must give particular attention to coping for
without this attention we cannot hope to understand how the
stress process works (Lazarus, 1998). To Lazarus coping is one of
two essential concepts the other being appraisal. So, we come to
the role of *coping* in Lazarus's transactional theory of stress. The
concept of coping has been around for a long time (Lazarus,
1993a). While the basic idea can be traced back to around
1400ad (Lazarus 1998), it was not until 1967 that the term
"coping" was given a separate category by *Psychological Abstracts*
(Snyder and Dinoff, 1999). In his autobiography, Lazarus (1998)
describes how his pioneering work on coping began at a time
when there was very little enthusiasm for the topic. His ideas and
research on coping first appeared in his 1966 book. Interest in
coping was, in the beginning, slow to develop, but this was to
change in the 1970s when coping research seemed to take off

with such enthusiasm that by 1994–7, 3,760 articles alone were published on coping (Snyder and Dinoff, 1999).

The late 1970s saw a shift in emphasis away from the more traditional view of coping as a trait or style, towards coping as a process (Lazarus, 1993a). While both perspectives are essential for a proper understanding of coping, each deals with a different issue with a trait approach focusing on stability and structure and a process approach focusing on change over time. Lazarus (1999) suggests that his process view of coping was one of his most important contributions to stress research. It was this view that formed the main focus of his field research. Along with his colleagues in the *Berkeley Stress and Coping Project* in the 1980s, the search was soon under way for a means to operationalizing this view and to begin to apply these measures to the lives of those whom they were studying.

There are, Lazarus suggested (see 1998, p.201), three principles of coping when viewed as a process. These are: *first*, that coping constantly changes over the course of an encounter; *secondly*, that coping must be assessed as independent of its outcomes; and *thirdly*, that coping consists of what an individual thinks and does in an effort to deal with the demands that tax or exceed resources. With these three principles in mind coping was defined as "constantly changing cognitive and behavioral efforts to manage specific external and/or internal demands that are appraised as taxing or exceeding the resources of the person" (Lazarus, 1998, p.201).

Ways of Coping Questionnaire

These three process principles of coping led, in the late 1970s and 1980s, the Berkeley Stress and Coping Project to create a procedure for measuring the coping process referred to as the *Ways of Coping Questionnaire* (see Folkman and Lazarus, 1980). The original questionnaire was made up of 68 items describing, a wide range of cognitive and behavioral strategies that people used (Folkman, Lazarus, Dunkel-Schetter, DeLongis, and Gruen, 1986) to manage the demands of a stressful encounter. The items were developed in accord with the theoretical model suggested by Lazarus (1966) and his colleagues (Lazarus and Launier, 1978) and from the coping literature. The questionnaire allowed only "yes" or "no" responses and was "always answered with a specific stressful event in mind" (Folkman, 1982, p.100).

Revisions to the original questionnaire (see Folkman and Lazarus, 1985) resulted in redundant and unclear items being removed, new items being added and the response format being changed to a 4-point scale ranging from "0 = does not apply and/or not used" to "3 = used a great deal." Aldwin (2000) was a member of the Berkeley Stress and Coping Project when it was decided to switch to a four-point scale. She records how "they agonised for some time over how to word the rating scale" (p.124) given the range of overlapping constructs like effort, frequency and duration. "We could not untangle this Gordian knot, and thus fell back on using the admittedly very subjective and vague term 'extent to which you used each strategy.' However we felt strongly enough that the amount of coping effort expended was too important to ignore, despite the fuzziness that it added to the scale" (p.124). This difficulty was a reflection of the debate that was eventually to follow the use of questionnaires to measure coping.

The revised questionnaire became the most widely used measure in research on coping (Lazarus, 1998). The questionnaire made possible and was designed to provide "a process, contextually oriented approach to coping" (Lazarus, 1993a, p.237). It could be used interactively during an interview or as a self-administered procedure, where individuals responded to the different items. The questionnaire asked whether and to what extent a person had used certain thoughts and actions in a particular stressful encounter. The items in the questionnaire were classified into two categories (see Folkman and Lazarus, 1980). The *problem-focused* category included items "that describe cognitive problem-solving efforts and behavioral strategies for altering or managing the source of the problem" (1980, p.224). The *emotion-focused* category included "cognitive and behavioral efforts directed at reducing or managing emotional distress" (1980, p.225). Because this "classification did not reflect the complexity and richness of coping processes, a series of factor analyses with different data sets were carried out, generating over time" (Schwarzer and Schwarzer, 1996, p.114) eight empirically derived coping scales (see, for example, Lazarus 1999, p.115).

These eight coping scales were, over time, found to be relatively consistent and helpful (Lazarus, 1999).

The pace at which coping research was to develop is nothing short of awesome (Lazarus, 1999). Citing a number of studies that drew on the Lazarus-Folkman approach, and reflecting on the fact that these are probably representative of many more not cited, Lazarus identified, in the space of a page-and-a-half in his 1999 book, 83 "significant" coping studies, many employing the *Ways of Coping Questionnaire* (pp.118–19). The volume of research on coping is a theme taken up earlier, by Lazarus and Folkman (1987) when they described how they, together with a number of other investigators, began in the late 1970s to develop, in earnest process measures of coping.

Lazarus and Folkman went on to identify four teams of researchers who were, at that time, developing coping inventories, and by the time Schwarzer and Schwarzer conducted their survey of coping instruments in 1996 they could identify 12 coping inventories in common use in addition to the *Ways of Coping Questionnaire*. From this volume of work and through his reviews of process studies, Lazarus (1993; 1999), was to identify "five empirical generalizations, all of which have been replicated numerous times by ourselves and others" (1999, p.119). These include (see Lazarus, 1999, pp.119–22): (a) people use a range of coping strategies in every stressful encounter, (b) some coping strategies are tied to personality variables, whereas others are tied to the social context, (c) coping strategies change from one time to another as the encounter unfolds, (d) secondary appraisals of control influence the selection of a coping strategy, and (e) coping is a powerful mediator of the emotional outcome.

The volume of research on coping, based around the use of coping questionnaires, has produced some of the most trenchant criticism with writers referring to "the mindlessly repetitive use of these instruments" (Coyne, 1997, p.153), and the "continued and misguided dominance of the psychometric approach in applied coping research (Somerfield, 1997, p.175). Lazarus was well aware of the issues facing researchers when it came to measuring coping, particularly when questionnaires were the primary method of data collection. From the early 1990s, Lazarus had already begun to question the almost exclusive reliance on questionnaires in coping research.

While questionnaires were, Lazarus (1998) suggested, useful for collecting certain kinds of data, and in no way wanting to "trash" the *Ways of Coping Questionnaire* as an approach to coping measurement, questionnaires tend to overlook meaning. They were not, Lazarus (1998) argued, capable of, nor, in fairness, were they designed to capture the richness and complexity of the coping process. Important as they were, in terms of the insights they did provide, they had barely begun to scratch the surface in the pursuit for a much fuller understanding of the coping process. On two occasions, when commenting on the state of coping research (1997; 2000), Lazarus argued in favor of more in-depth studies of the coping process, noting how encouraged he was by the growing number of resourceful researchers committed to identifying alternative methods to better understand the nature of coping and who were investigating coping in more detail using in-depth, longitudinal, and more holistic methods (Lazarus, 2000). This view is now "the emerging consensus and the time is ripe to give alternative approaches a try" (Somerfield, 1997, p.176).

Lazarus and Emotions

Lazarus (2001) talks in terms of his work progressing through three phases: (a) the origins and terminology of the appraisal construct, (b) appraisal theory as applied to psychological stress, and (c) a change in focus from stress to emotions. Lazarus had always sensed the importance of emotions, and as early as 1966 had began paying attention to emotion theory. For some time stress and emotions had been treated as two "quite independent literatures" and "really should be dealt with as a single unified topic. Emotion is, in effect, a superordinate concept, and stress is a subordinate but very important part of the emotional life" (Lazarus, 2001, p.54). The link between appraisal and emotions was routed through the idea of *core relational meanings*, where every emotion was linked to a different pattern of appraisals (Lazarus, 2001). The difficulties and complexities when dealing with emotions are considerable and well discussed by Lazarus (1991; 1993; 1999; 2001). What is important from Lazarus's point of view is that when thinking about appraisal and emotions, we think of them in terms of an emotional whole. Most appraisal theories are good at distinguishing the components of meaning from emotions, but they are not so good at describing the pathway that brings them together, linked as they are, through core relational meanings (Lazarus, 1999). Taking this to a higher level of abstraction requires that each emotion is associated with a core relational theme. The debate surrounding appraising and appraisals, emotions and core relational themes have been touched on and discussed above. While there is much to consider in what Lazarus has given, through his core relational meanings as a causal pathway, this may well provide researchers with the organizing concept that is so desperately needed in stress research to herald in what may be new beginnings and new methods ready to take such ideas forward.

Summary

It would be difficult to sum up what is 50 years of research if the work of Lazarus hadn't made such a fundamental contribution. A full account of the research and theory of Richard Lazarus can be found in his 1998a book where he provides what he describes as "an analysis of historical and perennial issues." The Berkeley Stress and Coping Project in all its three incarnations spanned some 30 years. Today, some 15 years after it ended, the work that Lazarus and his colleagues produced on appraisal, coping, and emotions is still at the heart of stress research. The fact that the debate surrounding some of these concepts is still intense reflects the theoretical and methodological challenges that Lazarus and his colleagues dared stress researchers to take up and embody in their work. His writings on the quality of coping research, his numerous calls for analysis and synthesis, his discussion of exemplary research designs, and his pleasure in finding an increasing amount of high quality and creative research that stress researchers can be proud of, seemed recognition enough for his principled stand against the restrictive characteristics of traditional methods.

Lazarus (2000) reacted modestly when being described as a leader in the field. "I would like to believe" he wrote " that I have described here a meaningful conceptual analysis and a workable set of methodological principles that could and should be tried out and ultimately judged heuristically" (Lazarus, 1998a, p.216). Lazarus has left us much more than that for the history of stress, and stress research has simply been enriched by his enormously powerful, thoughtful, and passionate contribution.

CHAPTER FIVE

Work Stress and Occupational Health Psychology

Introduction

In their seminal article on job stress and employee health, Beehr and Newman (1978) commented that as most people spend around half their waking lives at work, then it is more than likely that work factors will have an important influence on their well-being. A rich history of work stress was already in the making by the time Beehr and Newman wrote their article. The work stress research that began to appear in the 1950s and 1960s, was simply following a tradition that had its roots in the work on fatigue and mental hygiene, was molded by the requirements of two World Wars, and reflected changes in social and economic circumstances that created considerable opportunities for applied psychological research at work. The decades immediately after World War II reflected a spirit of optimism and innovation, but they were also marked by periods of industrial unrest and conflict (Cooper et al., 2001). The organizational culture that was to emerge from this time soon had commentators talking of the stresses and strains at work, and a need to systematically investigate the consequences of work-related stress.

Work Stress

By 1959, a research program exploring the work environment and mental health had been set up at the Institute for Social Research at the University of Michigan. However, even before this program had begun Zander and Quinn (1962) were able to find 75 studies that the Institute had been involved in, since 1948, that "contained empirical findings and theoretical speculations relevant to problems of mental health" (Kahn and French, 1962, p.122). While these studies became the research ancestry of the program begun in 1959, they had really only scratched the surface of the problem in a variety of contexts. By 1962, a review of the Institute's current work led to the conclusion that "the industrial environment has powerful effects on the mental and physical health of the person" (Kahn and French, pp.126-7), and that these effects represented a major social problem. The study that was to emerge from the Institute's program, and which was to thrust their work onto center stage, was the study carried out by Kahn and his colleagues into the nature, causes and consequences of two types of organizational stress: *role conflict* and *role ambiguity* (Kahn, Wolfe, Quinn, Snoek, and Rosenthal, 1964).

Kahn and his colleagues (1964) described how their work stemmed from the increasing growth in importance in the 1960s of organizations in shaping individual and social life. These organizational structures demanded a level of conformity and performance that reflected, in part, the new wave of management ideas about motivation, satisfaction, and leadership. To these researchers, the demands on workers to perform under conditions of ceaseless and accelerating change were fertile ground for problems like conflict and ambiguity, and so "to the costly ideology of bureaucratic conformity is added the irony of conflicting and ambiguous directions" (Kahn et al., 1964, p.6). Conflict and ambiguity, these authors were to argue, are not simply infuriating, but in the extreme they are identity destroying. At its simplest level, *role conflict* was defined as the "simultaneous occurrence of two (or more) sets of pressures such that compliance with one would make more difficult compliance with the other" (Kahn et al., 1964, p.19). *Role ambiguity* was conceived as the "extent to which required information is available to a given organizational position" (Kahn et al., 1964, p.25). Where such information is lacking, the individual will experience ambiguity. Both role conflict and role ambiguity were associated with emotional turmoil. The pioneering work of Kahn and his colleagues, and the insights their theoretical approach provided, was to mark the beginning of work stress research.

Role Conflict, Role Ambiguity, and the Search for Causes of Work Stress

Role conflict and role ambiguity came to dominate the early history of work stress. Then, as now, despite well over a decade of persistent and growing criticism, they were and probably still are, the most frequently measured causes of work stress. The intensive interview protocol that accompanied the work of Kahn (1964) and his colleagues produced rather modest measures of role conflict and role ambiguity (King and King, 1990). However, their theoretical work, their first attempts to operationalized these constructs, and the directions they provided for future research ushered in a rich and fruitful period of exploration and investigation. The work by Rizzo, House, and Lirtzman in 1972 produced the first self-report measures of role conflict and role ambiguity. These authors developed, from the theoretical parameters establish by Kahn and his colleagues, 15 statements that dealt with role conflict and 15 that dealt with role ambiguity. Respondents were asked to indicate, on a seven-point Likert-type scale the degree to which the condition existed for them. Analysis of the items showed that role conflict and role ambiguity emerged as separate dimensions. The work that followed by House and Rizzo (1972) entitled "Role conflict and role ambiguity as critical variables in a model of organizational behaviour" "helped keep researcher's attention on them for almost two decades" (Beehr, 1995, p.55).

By 1981, Van Sell, Brief, and Schuler were to comment that a psychometric evaluation of the role conflict and role ambiguity scales developed by Rizzo et al. (1972) "suggests high construct validity and continued use" (Van Sell, Brief, and Schuler, 1981, p.64). By the time Fisher and Gitelson published their meta-analysis in 1983, they were able to identify 43 'role conflict–role ambiguity' studies, and by 1985, Jackson and Schuler using the same technique, were able to find almost 200 role conflict–role ambiguity studies. However, the conclusions drawn by these reviewers, more often reflected the view, that while the volume of research on role conflict and role ambiguity may be impressive "it is disheartening to note that few conclusions can be drawn and the lack of specificity with which they must be stated" (Van Sell, Brief, and Schuler, 1981, p.66). There also seemed to be, at this time, a growing consensus among the reviewers that the impact of role conflict and role ambiguity would be better understood by exploring the moderating influence of individual and organizational variables on the relationship between role conflict, role ambiguity, and well-being. There was, all these reviewers were to conclude, much work to be done in terms of scale refinement and development, research design, and understanding the context from which role expectations emerge.

Discussion surrounding the validity, reliability, and what exactly it was that the Rizzo et al (1972) role conflict and role ambiguity scales were, and should be measuring, continued throughout the 1980s and into the 1990s. There were, however, as Jex (1998, p.13) makes clear, "few attempts to develop alternative measures" of these constructs. However, as we shall see later, the development by Cooper, Sloan and Williams (1988) of the *Occupational Stress Indicator* was to have a significant effect on the diagnosis of work stress. Debate surrounding how best work stressors should be measured did not, as we shall see, confine itself to role related measures. The debate was to broaden out into one reminiscent of the measurement debates of the past. No less significant in its intensity, and in the eloquence of the points made, work stress, like any other facet of stress research, cannot escape the history that has preceded it or the obligations it imposes on contemporary researchers. The continued focus, by many researchers on role conflict and role ambiguity was to produce a side effect that was to have a lasting influence on work stress research. The attention given to these two stressors seemed to signal to many researchers that there was little need to focus on other potential stressors, and the emphasis given to role conflict and role ambiguity appeared to be for no other reason "other than they were early arrivals" (Beehr, 1995, p.55).

There was another role stressor that was to hold the attention of work stress researchers: *role overload*. Kahn (1964) and his colleagues were to point to role overload as "standing out as another type of role conflict confronting sizable numbers in the labor force" (p.59). Role overload was described in terms of the amount of work to do in the time available. Overload, as Kahn (1964) and his colleagues suggested, was experienced when a person was faced with deciding which tasks, within the given time limits, to comply with and which to hold off. The pressure that this creates and the difficulties of deciding how to comply may, argued Kahn (1964) and his colleagues, tax individuals beyond the limits of their ability. It was not just the amount of work that was a problem there was also the added difficulty of getting the work done and satisfying quality standards as well. By 1970, Sales was referring not just to role overload but role underload as common features of American organizational life. Role underload he described as the condition where individuals are faced with task requirements that require considerably less time to do than the time available. Role underload, Sales (1970) was to conclude, may be stressful "because of its presumably boring and uninteresting characteristics" (p.593).

At the same time, Kahn was also arguing for a set of concepts that capture the extent to which "the atrophy caused by the underutilization, and the breakage caused by overload are really measuring the same kind of thing, stresses damaging to the system" (Kahn, 1970, p.102). Kahn also drew attention to the difference between quantitative overload (too much work to do in the time available) and qualitative overload (the demands of the job becoming more difficult and exceeding individual skills and abilities), suggesting that here was another distinction that had, typically not been taken into account. By the mid 1970s, self-report measures of role overload were in use (see Beehr, Walsh, and Taber, 1976). Generally, these scales measured the demands of the job in terms of the time constraints to get things done, the quantity of work to do, and the difficulties of meeting performance standards. Later scale development (see Jex, 1998; Spector, Dwyer, and Jex, 1988) added items to measure underload (amount of free time) and quality (how often you do work that you really don't know how to do). Despite the popularity of self-report measures of role overload, argued Jex, "there are undoubtedly other ways to measure role overload" including "some combination of objective and subjective measures" (1988, pp.15, 16). Interestingly, work by Narayanan, Menon, and Spector (1999), using a stress incident record, found that work overload was still being reported as a source of stress far more frequently than role conflict and role ambiguity.

Beyond Role Conflict, Ambiguity, and Overload

The late 1970s produced work that was to raise the focus and extend our understanding of the range of work stressors. There were the seminal articles by Cooper and Marshall (1976), and in the following years Beehr and Newman (1978), and the book by Cox (1978). Beehr and Newman (1978) were, through their use of facet analysis, able to identify four major facets of work stressors. These included job demands and task characteristics, role demands or expectations, organizational characteristics and conditions, and organization's external demands and conditions. What was particularly telling from their analysis was that these four facets covered 37 potential causes of work stress. Even more telling, was that of these 37 causes, only five (weekly work schedule, over and under utilization of skills, role overload, role conflict, and company size) had, at that time, been investigated in terms of the job stress-employee health domain. The Cooper and Marshall (1976) and the Beehr and Newman (1978) article were to become two of the most frequently cited articles from the 1970s. They heralded an explosion of research that in the 27 years from 1970 to 1997 saw 2870 cited under the heading *occupational stress* in the indices of *Psychological Abstracts* (Beehr, 1998, p.839). Yet a close examination of those figures suggests that it was not until the late 1980s that work stress research began to flourish.

Reflecting back on the mid to late 1970s, Beehr (1998) speculated on why, despite the work of Kahn and his colleagues, work stress had not, some 14 years after their work was first published, established itself as a significant area of study in organizational psychology. Beehr found a curious resistance on the part of researchers to welcoming this new topic to the discipline. However, as he suggested, the detail and model they provided in the 1978 article, practically begged researchers to investigate the ready-made hypotheses they provided. This was to become an invitation many researchers couldn't resist, and although there have been considerable advances in work stress research since 1978; it is "still an unfinished enterprise" (Beehr, 1998, p.843).

At around the same time, Cooper and Marshall (1976) published their study that identified six major categories of work stressors. These included factors intrinsic to the job, role in the organization, career development, organizational structure and climate, relationships at work, and extra-organizational sources of stress. This was, to these authors, a first step towards providing for researchers an integrated framework and conceptual map for considering more systematically the sources of work stress. The book by Cox (1978) also made a substantial contribution to the development of work stress research. From the chapter coauthored by Mackay they produced a similar list that reinforced the view that to understand the debilitating nature of work stress, we must first understand what causes it, and from that platform move towards its prevention and treatment. Cooper, Beehr, and Cox continue to make their mark on work stress research. Many reviews were to follow (see, for example, Beehr, 1995; Glowinkowski and Cooper, 1987; Jex and Beehr, 1991; Kahn and Byosiere, 1992; Kinicki, McKee, and Wade, 1996; Schuler, 1980) with authors identifying similar categories of work stressors. Many of these reviews now however, were to reflect a subtle shift in emphasis. No longer content to present a list of work stressors many reviewers began to draw attention to the methodological difficulties associated with measuring work stressors. So by the mid-to-late 1980s work stress researchers simply became captives of the past and, like researchers before them, were drawn into discussing measurement issues.

If it is true, as Beehr suggests, that measurement problems in job stress research "seem truly to know no bounds" (1995, p.231), then this may help explain why, many researchers, treat such discussions seriously but somewhat indifferently, leaving others to act on them rather than building them into their own research. These issues are, however, as much a part of our history as the arguments that surround them. Their significance in shaping the future will in no way be lessened by restating them one more time. Despite all the reviews and the wide range of stressors identified, there is still this lingering concern that work stress researchers have, for too long, been preoccupied with the measurement of role conflict and role ambiguity. This concern was, over time, to develop into the view that while the reliability of these scales continued to be obediently reported and emphasized, this was at the expense of their relevance (see Cooper et al., 2001). By failing to take into account the significant social and economic change that had occurred since the measures were first developed, researchers may now be overstating the significance of these events, ignoring the presence of others and failing to consider other more salient events (Brief and Atieh, 1987; Glowinkowski and Cooper, 1985).

At the same time, other researchers (see Cooper et al., 2001; DeFrank, 1988) were suggesting that, the assessment of work stressors might have been oversimplified, as measures invariably failed to capture their frequency, duration, demand, intensity, and meaning, nor the causal relationship between different stressors, thereby failing to describe their accumulative effect. While there was a general consensus that more needed to be done in terms of measurement practice to better understand the nature of work stressors, that consensus was not apparent when Perrewe and Zellars (1999) suggested that cognitive appraisal has been ignored by much of the current empirical stress research. The debate around subjective versus objective measurement (Frese and Zapf, 1999; Schaubroeck, 1999) of work stressor measurement, is as robust now, as the debates that have preceded it.

Nevertheless despite the indifference by some researchers to move beyond cross-sectional, self-report designs preferring others to lead the way then other researchers have done just that. More and more researchers are leading the way in terms of creative research designs by combining the strengths of the qualitative and quantitative traditions to produce daily process designs, which include daily diary recording, momentary sampling, the analysis of narratives, the use of longitudinal analysis and time intensive designs, and the application of process design research with its strong association with clinical practice.

Early Research Frameworks and Identifying Strains

Identifying work stressors ran parallel with considering their impact or outcome. In the beginning, work stress research, quite naturally began, by using a simple correlational framework, to investigate the relationship between work stressors (stimuli, S) and strain (response, R). This S–R approach was important historically, for it led to three types of research. These included (see Cooper et al. 2001; Dewe, 1991; 2001) identifying, describing, and categorizing different work stressors, exploring the relationship between the different work stressors and a range of strains (responses) and, eventually to exploring those organizational, situational, and individual variables that may moderate the stimulus–response relationship. Describing these different types of research in this way, is not meant to reflect any sort of orderly progression. Researchers were to follow their own paths and establish their own goals and directions, as different interests and issues attracted their attention. This is particularly true when you search for some history in terms of the strain (response) side of this framework.

Since Kahn (1964) and his colleagues first talked about tensions, dissatisfactions, and inner conflicts, a wide variety of strains have been associated with work stress. In their 1979 article, Beehr and Newman identified under their heading of *Human Consequences Facet* – psychological health consequences, physical health consequences, and behavioral consequences (1979, pp.672-3). Since that time most major reviews have classified job related strains under those three headings – psychological, physiological, and behavioral. Just as earlier researchers may have searched for general or more specific responses to stress, the search for the *effects* of work stress has been influenced, not so much by an indiscipline on the part of researchers to measure whatever pleases them, but by the fact that being under stress meant that virtually any strain or response could be described as a stress response. This has led to considerable ambiguity as to what we mean when we talk about "being under stress," and a division, among researchers, as to how worthwhile the term "stress" really is. While we will return to the question of "what do we mean by stress," it is clear that researchers have, over the years, "only paid moderate attention to delineating the strain side of the stress transaction" (Cooper et al., 2001, p.72).

The cost of regarding any response as a stress response, means that our understanding of whether some work stressor produces specific effects has not advanced. Some stressors may be described as having little or no effect, when it may be more likely that the "wrong" effects have been measured. In addition, few attempts have been made to consider what type of response might be anticipated in different contexts. It is also necessary to move, as Kahn and Byosiere (1992) suggest, from the more generic categories of strains to a more detailed understanding of the nature of strains, in terms of whether they are acute or chronic, reflect over or under stimulation, and reflect more general or specific feelings. Alternatively, job-related burnout (see Cooper et al., 2001) has a long history in relation to the human service professions, and its measurement and correlates are well established. Not so in the case of emotions. Even though, as Ashforth and Humphrey suggest, "the experience of work is saturated with emotions, research has generally neglected the impact of everyday emotions on organizational life" (1995, p.97).

Several reasons have been given for this state of affairs. These range from the view that "emotions have little to do with, and even get in the way of, the proper legitimate and highly successful business-like business of work" (Briner, 1995, p.3) to all too frequently, emotions are confounded with attitudes. If, as Lazarus (1999) makes clear, emotions offer a rich pathway for understanding what is happening to a person, then this may offer researchers the organizing concept for exploring in a more systematic way the impact of work stressors. By the late 1990s this challenge seems to have been taken up as researchers tackle the theory, research, and management of emotions at work and begin to develop a more specific interest in the role of positive emotions at work like, for example, happiness and a general concern for the development of a more positive psychology that explores "what makes a good life."

Towards an Integrated Model of Work Stress

As already noted, the correlational-interactional (S-R) model of work stress provided researchers with a wealth of information, and enabled them to achieve what many saw as their first priority: to identify different work stressors and to consider their impact on employee health and well-being. At times, in order to better understand the stressor–strain relationship, researchers explored whether it was moderated by different social, situational, or individual variables. This latter approach provided researchers, when some form of moderated relationship was found, with a basis to speculate on the nature of those processes that may be involved. This interactional approach soon outlived its usefulness. It was neither designed, nor capable, of providing a framework for explaining the stress process, and therefore could not support a theory of stress (Lazarus, 1990). Models of work stress have, however, long contained elements of process (see Cooper et al., 2001). Researchers have also acknowledged, at least at the theoretical level, a transactional view of stress (Lazarus, 1966), although many still prefer to research work stress using an interactional perspective. This preference, Lazarus argues, means that while work stress is regarded as important, researchers continue to pay only "lip service to the most advanced theories about the stress process" (1991, p.2). In an attempt to unravel this state of affairs, some historical analysis follows.

In 1970, Kahn commented "we stand to learn most about stress by trying to follow that sequence of events through, in reasonably complete form, from environment to stress system" (p.99). Kahn then outlined the schema he and his colleagues had been using at the Institute for Social Research (ISR) at the University of Michigan (see French and Kahn, 1962). Beginning with some demand from the external environment that is then recognized or received by the person, the individual responds. Distinguishable from the immediate response are what "what might be called the enduring consequences or longer-range effects, of stress and the response to it" (Kahn, 1970, p.99). Kahn made clear the importance of following this sequential approach as a pragmatic goal. Embodied in this schema were issues of perception, the appropriateness and adequacy of the response and the capacity of the individual to react. Perhaps one of the most telling points made by Kahn (1970), was that as researchers cannot investigate everything, choices have to be made, and priorities determined about what aspects of the process will be emphasized. We need to avoid, argued Kahn (1970), getting those priorities defined into what we mean by stress and, as a result, researching a narrower concept than was first intended. Perhaps in the rush to research workplace stress, some choices eventually failed to improve our research in a way that had been hoped.

The ISR model "is straightforward, easy to understand, and has guided much of the work stress research and theorizing in the past 25 years" (Jex and Beehr, 1991, p.313). The usefulness of the ISR model lies, as Jex and Beehr (1991) point out, in reminding researchers that stress is a multistaged process. However, as they go on to suggest, many researchers have chosen to ignore this feature of the model, preferring instead to simply correlate work stressors with different responses; a research design that offers little understanding of the processes involved (Jex and Beehr, 1991). Kahn's (1970) description of the ISR model came from a paper he presented at a conference in 1967. The purpose of this conference "was to identify crucial issues in the area of social-psychological stress and to seek potential research approaches to those issues" (McGrath, 1970, p.v). In drawing together "some strategic considerations for future research on social-psychological stress" at the end of the conference, McGrath identified as the first strategic directive, "the need to approach the problem of stress systematically, with a set of concepts that encompasses the full sequence of events and with an approach aimed at seeking the linkages among the parts of this sequence" (McGrath, 1970, p.348). The scene was set for a number of researchers to take up this challenge.

Of all the models in the work stress literature, the most widely discussed is the *person–environment* (P–E) fit model. This model, a product of the ISR program, presents a "*quantitative* approach to adjustment and coping," where *adjustment* is perceived "as the goodness of fit between the characteristics of the person and the properties of the environment" (French, Rodger, and Cobb 1974, p.316). The P–E fit model emphasizes the interrelationship between the person and the environment, "and the complex processes which underlie this relationship" (Van Harrison, 1978, p.202). In brief, this model proposes that strain occurs when there is a misfit between the person and the environment, that is, when this P–E relationship is out of equilibrium. Two types of fit are identified. The first refers to a *needs–supplies* misfit (opportunities to meet those needs), where as the second describes a *demand–abilities misfit* (Caplan, 1983). Embedded in the notion of misfit is the individual's ability to manage the encounter. Despite extensions and refinements to this model (Caplan, 1983; Van Harrison, 1978), there are still considerable difficulties in clarifying the precise nature of misfit (Edwards and Cooper, 1988). Although broadly cited, as Eulberg, Weekley, and Bhagat point out; it is still the ISR model that preceded it that has generated "an enormous amount of research" (1988, p.336).

In 1978, Beehr and Newman proposed their general model of stress. Their model is "general enough to be a framework for most approaches to and research on job stress" (Beehr and Franz, 1987, p.11). One of the important aspects of the Beehr and Newman model is their "process facet" of psychological and physical processes that is initiated in any stressful encounter. These process facets they describe, are those activities within the indi-vidual "which transform input (stimuli)" and "produce output (consequences)" (Beehr and Newman, 1978, p.681), and include, for example, "appraisal of the situation" and "decision making regarding an appropriate response". The aim of their proposals was to motivate researchers towards developing a more system-atic approach to the field of work stress. Other work stress models were to follow including, for example, the stress cycle model (McGrath, 1976), the job demand–job control model (Karasek, 1979), the general systems approach (Cox and McKay, 1981), and the cybernetic model of Cummings and Cooper (1979). These models and others (see Cooper, 1998) have a number of notable points of convergence (Kahn and Byosiere, 1991). These include a demanding encounter, the recognition that the encoun-ter is significant and consequences that affect the well-being of the individual.

The fundamental premise that characterizes all these models is that strain occurs when there is a misfit, mismatch or imbalance between the demands of the encounter and the resources of the individual. The dilemma facing researchers is to agree on the exact nature of that misfit or imbalance. One of the difficulties with work stress models is that "although they identify some of the structural components that precipitate a misfit, they fre-quently fail to identify those elements that characterize the nature of the misfit and that link the person and the environ-ment" (Cooper et al., 2001, p.19). While many researchers would agree that the misfit must be perceived as significant, represent some sort of threat to well-being, and require a response over and above normal functioning, there is still disagreement as to how these evaluations come about and how they should be measured. Agreeing the nature of the misfit is, for work stress researchers fundamental, as it focuses attention on process issues and draws attention to the transactional nature of stress.

Lazarus (1991) makes it clear that adopting a transactional approach to work stress offers a very different approach than what he describes as the "static or structural approach," which is "indigenous to the field of industrial stress" (Lazarus, 1991, p.2). The debate as to the application of the transactional approach to work settings is not yet settled (see, for example, Barone, 1991; Brief and George, 1991; Dewe, 2001; Harris, 1991). The issues discussed and the points made "rather than disenfranchise the transactional model point to the need for more research, for researchers to consider alternative frameworks for exploring the stress process and to consider the impact of such issues on traditional measurement and analysis" (Dewe, 2001, p.72). One aspect of the transactional model that has received attention from work stress researchers is the area of coping.

Work Stress and Coping

In their article "Whither stress research?: an agenda for the 1980s," Payne, Jick, and Burke (1982) noted, in terms of work stress and coping, "detailed attention to this problem is beginning to pay off and a few measures of coping style are now available," and concluded that "the coping component of the stress process is still another 'piece' of the puzzle worth examining" (p.141). Almost 20 years later pointing to the "boundless enthusiasm for coping research seen in the 1980s," Somerfield and McCrae (2000) suggested that this enthusiasm had been replaced by what they described as "widespread disaffection, intense scrutiny, and corresponding calls for change" (p.620). There was certainly, in the intervening years, no shortage of advice as to the direction coping research should take, nor was there any difficulty in identifying the issues that needed addressing. So what has happened to coping research for it to be described in this way? We begin our historical account by taking "coping measurement" as our theme from a varied and large coping literature.

The history of research into coping with work stress appears to be mainly taxonomic (Cox, 1987), where researchers described and categorized coping behaviors that were broadly applicable to all work situations. It is too the seminal work of Kahn (1964) and his colleagues that we turn first. Part of their intensive interview program focused on *"experienced stress and coping techniques"* (p.443). They used open-ended questions such as "when you get into a situation of stress or exceptional pressure, what do you usually do to handle the situation?" and "when the tension is really pretty strong, what do you do to get it out of your system?" to explore the issue of coping. Their aim was not to provide, what they called a "grab-bag of coping mechanisms from which one can pick and choose the appropriate device next time he [sic] is under stress" (1964, p.338), but to present through six individual case studies coping examples that illustrated the overall picture.

Kahn (1964) and his colleagues provided a number of insights into coping, ensuring the historical importance of their work. From the outset they distinguished between coping styles and behaviors commenting, "the introduction of such a notion as style does not mean, however, that we are casting our lot wholly with those who maintain that an individual unvaryingly applies the same coping mechanism to varying stresses, rather than freely employing the solution which best fits the specific problem" (p.338). They also emphasized the importance of context, the characteristics of the core problem, personality issues and the costs of coping to individual well-being concluding "coping is defined by the behaviors subsumed under it, not by the success of such behaviors" (1964, p.340). Their work, and the earlier reporting of some of the coping data by Wolfe and Snoek (1962), set in place the framework for much of the work that was to follow. Their hope "that the effort and its product may contribute to the understanding of organized human behavior. We know of no more urgent problem" (Kahn et al., 1964, p.398) was well and truly realized.

The 1970s saw the first attempts to identify, in a work setting, coping strategies. Early work by Burke (1971) and Burke and Belcourt (1974), using an open-ended method similar to Kahn (1964) et al., asked "what ways have you personally found useful in handling the tensions and pressures of your jobs?" These authors provided a contingency model of coping responses, arguing that issues like how individuals learn, are socialized to use, and find new coping strategies, are complexities that have to be dealt with if a general approach to coping is to develop. These authors also provided, from their data, a list of coping strategies, and it was these results that were eventually to give shape to self-report coping questionnaires. The enthusiasm for coping research had begun. Researchers almost immediately became interested in issues like effective coping (Howard, Richnitzer, and Cunningham, 1975; Shalit, 1977), maladaptive coping (Hagen, 1978), their function (Pearlin and Schooler, 1978) and the most frequently used coping strategies (Kiev and Kohn,

1979). By the time Newman and Beehr (1979) published their second seminal paper at the end of the decade, the first "comprehensive and critical review of both personal and organizational strategies for handling job stress" (p.2) was available.

The expectation of Payne et al. (1982) that the 1980s would result in "an expanded commitment to stress research" because the "magnitude and complexity of the problem warrants this investment" (p.143) were certainly met when it came to coping research. This decade continued to see more and more studies attempting to identify and classify coping strategies. While open-ended questions (empirically driven approaches) were still being used to capture and describe what individuals actually thought and did, researchers were also turning to theory to guide the development of coping measures. A number of studies offered a methodical and detailed analysis of the coping literature, followed by a well-argued case why strategies were selected for inclusion in the measure (Feldman and Brett, 1983; Latack, 1986; Stone and Neale, 1984). This distinction between empirically based and theory-driven approaches, while important, does tend to mask the range of approaches that have been adopted to identify coping strategies. Nevertheless by the end of the decade work related coping scales had begun to emerge (e.g. Dewe and Guest, 1990; Latack, 1986; Schwartz and Stone, 1993). For many researchers though, the systematic development of a work-based coping measure, was not a primary objective. Researchers were, as has previously been noted, more interested and somewhat in a hurry to explore coping effectiveness, the influence of personality, gender, and age on coping, coping with specific work stressors, and coping styles versus coping behaviors. The effect of this sort of research was, however, to draw attention away from the more substantive measurement issues, towards issues of context and process without first putting in place, and building on, a proper understanding of how best to measure coping.

The 1980s and 1990s saw little pause in the number of work stress and coping articles published. However, despite all the energy and attention being given to coping research, this was a time when researchers began to voice some concern as to whether it was now time for a period of quiet reflection to consider where all this energy was taking research, and what could be said as to the amount of progress that had been made. One of the causes for this concern had been the considerable debate and discussion that was occurring around the classification of coping strategies (Dewe, 2000). The most popular approach has been to use the distinction first made by Lazarus and Folkman (1984) between "problem-focused" and "emotion-focused" strategies. This period saw several alternative classification schemes being proposed (see Cox and Ferguson, 1991; Dewe and Guest, 1990; Ferguson and Cox, 1997; Latack, 1986) "but these too do not appear to satisfy the precision required to encapsulate the different functions that coping strategies may perform or to adequately capture the range of potential coping responses" (Cooper et al., 2001, p.166). The inherent danger when attempting to classify coping strategies was in thinking that classifying coping strategies was the same as researching the coping process. Researchers soon began to realize that classifying a coping strategy as problem-focused or emotion-focused, was not quite so easy when considered within the context of the coping process, since in process terms it is not always clear as to how a particular coping strategy is actually being used.

It was also during this time, that reviewers began to question the way in which coping strategies were being measured, and began to suggest that perhaps "coping had become too narrowly method bound, defined by the uncritical application of standard checklists" (Coyne and Gottlieb, 1996, p.961). Rather than abandon coping checklists, other reviews (e.g. Dewe, 2001; Somerfield, 1997) pointed to a number of design issues that needed confronting if the full potential of coping checklists was to be realized. Others (e.g. Tennen, Affleck, Armeli, and Carney, 2000) were to argue for the use of alternative methods and pointed to the successful way in which qualitative techniques had been used to capture the richness of the coping process. Despite the debates, the intensity of feeling and at times the polarization of views, coping research was not "all about stubborn methodological problems and reviewers, although focusing on a number of theoretical and methodological issues are not short on possible solutions" (Dewe, 2001, p.64). There is, as Lazarus suggests "a growing number of sophisticated, resourceful and vigorous researchers who are dedicated to the study of coping" (2000, p.665).

From Coping to the Self-Help Years to Stress Management

Work stress has become part of what Beehr and Franz describe as "an object of massive scientific research" (1987, p.3). Work stress is as enthusiastically discussed in the popular literature, as it is in professional and scientific journals. It is not difficult to understand why stress has sometimes been described as something of its own industry. Despite the drawbacks that this popularity presents, the systematic presentation of the causes and consequences of stress, particularly stress at work, has meant that considerable attention has been directed towards the management and prevention of stress and a history of stress would not be complete without exploring these issues. Coping research with its emphasis on managing a stressful encounter, provided the climate for what became known as the *self-help* years.

Self-help techniques (e.g. exercise, relaxation, meditation, biofeedback, and a philosophy of life) began appearing in the 1960s, each with the aim of providing an inner sense of energy and well-being, and thus a greater capacity for dealing with and building resistance to stressful encounters. Often viewed as natural and innate protective mechanisms against stress or strategies for daily living each technique offers a programmed approach to improving our capacity to deal with stress. However, the potential of each technique and its relevance, depends on the commitment to the technique, and the fact that many of the techniques are advocating fundamental lifestyle changes and not simply suggesting that each becomes an add on in a time of stress. At the very least, they are simply part of a person's repertoire of coping, and their aim is not to get rid of stress but to develop an inner sense of energy for dealing with stress-related encounters.

Stress management was not just confined to those offering self-help programs. Kahn (1964) and his colleagues indicated in their work that while their emphasis had been on explaining the origins and consequences of role conflict and role ambiguity "the practitioners who reads these pages will do so with still a third consideration dominant in his [sic] mind: what can be done to reduce the incidence of role conflict and ambiguity, and to make the effects of these conditions minimally damaging to the person and to the organization" (p.386). Kahn and his colleagues suggested four ways, which would, in the case of role conflict and ambiguity not eliminate these conditions but make them "tolerable, and low in cost, and which at best might be positive in contribution to individuals and organizations" (p.387). The four ways included restructuring the organization, developing new selection criteria, increasing the individual's coping capacity, and strengthening the bond between organizational members.

In the years that followed the Kahn et al. (1964) study, there have "been hundreds of published research findings, newspaper and magazine articles, and books dealing with topics of 'executive neurosis,' 'blue collar blues,' 'white collar woes,' and other issues of occupational mental health" (Gavin, 1977, p.198). The sheer volume of published materials and available techniques and strategies led Gavin to ask "why so much concern about employee mental health *now*?" The answer it seems (Gavin, 1977, pp.198-9) lay, in what was across North America and Europe: growing concerns for a quality of working life, changing social attitudes towards mental illness, managers taking a more active role in areas like job stress, the passing of occupational health and safety legislation, and an enhanced appreciation of how different parts of society are interrelated and no part can be viewed in isolation. So, by the late 1970s, working arrangements had changed to such a "degree that a more holistic view of the person in the work setting is emerging" so that when the interplay between work and health is considered "we can see the ramifications for our future organizational society" – the development of "health promoting work environments" (Gavin, 1977, p.201). It was the late 1970s that saw the first systematic attempts at developing workplace stress interventions.

By 1977, Torrington and Cooper were suggesting a range of interventions that could come from the personnel specialists within the organization. They described these kinds of interventions as falling into two categories: *operational* – where existing personnel operations are modified to mitigate against stress, and *influential*–those areas of management policy that can be influenced by personnel specialists to reduce their potential for stress. In a similar vein, Quick and Quick (1979) described *level 1 preventions*, such as restructuring jobs, or refining roles, and *level II preventions*, where the focus was on individual techniques aimed at providing the individual with a means of dissipating stressful feelings before they became damaging. By the time that Newman and Beehr presented their second paper in 1979 on "Personnel and organizational strategies for handling job stress" they could, from their review, identify at least 52 studies that provided an overview of the work that was going on. They were to conclude that the challenges facing researchers and practitioners included the need for more evaluative research, recognition of the interplay between work and other life spheres, the impact of individual and situational differences in determining the effectiveness of stress management programs, and the need for industrial/organizational psychologists to devote their considerable skills and experience to an area that they had yet to enter in force.

Other reviews were to follow that capture the history of stress management interventions. In the five years following the review by Newman and Beehr (1979), Murphy was to note that "a number of published and unpublished studies have provided a more rigorous evaluation of the merits of worksite stress management programmes" (1984, p.2). Murphy's review focused on individual-oriented approaches (e.g. biofeedback, muscle relaxation, cognitive restructuring) for helping people cope with stress. Following his comprehensive review and analysis of the different studies, Murphy, describing the field as young and in "need of more demonstration studies," concluded, that although all studies were associated with positive results "there is a clear danger, however, of organizations offering stress management training to workers and making no attempt to improve work conditions which generate stress" (1984, p.13). Three years later, following another comprehensive review of organizational stress management training Murphy (1987) was to point to the added value that can be achieved by organizations making stress management training part of their overall stress prevention-reduction program, but again emphasizing that stress management reflects just one aspect of what must be a more holistic approach to the issue of workplace stress.

The following year, in an even more comprehensive review of employee assistance programs (EAPs), stress management training, and stressor reduction strategies, Murphy was to conclude, by first pointing to stress prevention as a field of scientific inquiry still in its infancy, that stress "interventions that are comprehensive and address individual and organizational factors hold the greatest promise for effective reduction and prevention of stress at work" (1988, p.332). By 1995, Murphy and his colleagues (Hurrell, Sauter, and Keita) were to produce, from contributions to the 1992 conference on *Stress in the 90s: A changing workforce in a changing workplace*, an edited text covering an extensive array of topics examining interventions at the individual, organizational and policy levels with the aim of producing a new generation of research and discussion. At the same time as Murphy and his colleagues were making their mark on the field, others were doing the same.

The text by Quick and Quick (1984) on *Organizational Stress and Preventive Management* was to provided researchers with a framework for identifying points for possible preventive management intervention. Quick and Quick (1984, pp.151–3) described these as *primary prevention* aimed at eliminating or reducing the impact of risk factors (e.g. work stressors), *secondary prevention* aimed at reducing the intensity of the stress response, and *tertiary prevention* where the concern is with symptom detection aimed at alleviating discomfort and restoring effective functioning. This framework was to become, for the field at large, the standard approach when discussing the different levels of intervention. Quick and Quick (1984), like other researchers were concerned that any intervention strategy should be balanced not leaving individuals to manage unnecessarily. In another comprehensive review, Quick, Horn, and Quick (1987) were to place their intervention framework in a preventive medicine context to broaden out stress research to identify "effective stress prevention and intervention methods that need to be developed so that positive health consequences can occur at both the individual and organizational levels" (1987, p.34). The work by Quick and Quick in 1997, together with their colleagues (Nelson and Hurrell), provided for those interested in the development of the field a comprehensive and systematic account for practicing healthy prevention stress management.

Further substantive reviews and frameworks discussed by Ivancevich and Matteson (1987) and Ivancevich, Matteson, Freedman, and Phillips (1990) confirmed, "during the last decade, our knowledge of stress management interventions has increased substantially" (Ivancevich et al., 1990, p.252). Yet these reviewers, like others, were also concerned that although progress had been made, even more knowledge was required, as organizational environments grow increasingly more complex. The challenge they argued is to do better and for organizational psychologists to apply to this field the rigor and expertise that there research training has provided. All reviewers from the early 1980s onwards voiced concerns about the need for a balanced approach noting that for many organizations the preference was for " 'post hoc' individual-directed interventions" that seemed to contribute to a "rather one-sided approach" (Kompier and Cooper, 1999, p.2). Adopting a transactional perspective, Lazarus (1991c) was to argue, when it comes to stress management, means that the individual cannot be divorced from the environment as both are intimately linked in any encounter. To ignore one is to fail to understand the basis of any stressful transaction, and the focus on which stress management interventions should be based.

In addition to the issues raised by many of these reviews, others were to question the motives as to why organizations introduce stress management programs (Briner, 1997), how concerned managers really are about work stress (Daniels, 1996), and what role outside experts should play in any stress management program (Sunderland and Cooper, 2000). These questions simply reinforced the Ivancevich et al. (1990) dictum that as more becomes known about stress management interventions, so too does our thirst for more knowledge and a better understanding. Progress, as the different reviewers note, was being made. In amongst all this progress was the influential work of Cooper, Sloan, and Williams (1988) and their development of the *Occupational Stress Indicator* (OSI) – a diagnostic instrument that offered organizations a means by which they can "regularly audit and monitor organizational health and be proactive in stress reduction" (Cooper and Cartwright, 1994, p.467).

Widely used in Europe and the Far East, the OSI provided "a baseline measure, whereby stress reduction techniques can be evaluated" (Cooper and Cartwright, 1994, p.468). The use of the OSI could be extended to determine strategies for secondary interventions, and in terms of tertiary interventions, it can provide important data on the likelihood of take-up rates for different assistance programs. As Cooper and Cartwright make clear, the value of the OSI lies in the fact that it tailors "action to suit the assessed needs of the organization" and is therefore "more likely to be more effective than any 'broad brush' approach" (1994, p.464). The history of stress management, and those who have contributed to it, have come a long way towards achieving the goal of improving the quality of working life "so that all concerned – employees, organizations, and society as a whole – can benefit" (Ivancevich et al., 1990, p.260).

Occupational Health Psychology

The history of stress is also a history of occupational health psychology. The excellent "A history of occupational health psychology" by Barling and Griffiths (2003) is a graphic illustration of this. Their work moves from the early concerns with the dehumanizing world of work to the emergence of a discipline the aim of which is to "promote and protect the psychological and physical health of workers" (2003, p.30). Describing occupational health psychology as a "newly emerging field," Barling and Griffiths (2003, p.30) point to how quickly it has developed in a relatively short time. This progress they attribute to the work of researchers in England, Europe, and the United States. The momentum for this progress has, as Barling and Griffiths (2003) also suggest, been driven by institutions such as the National Institute for Occupational Safety and Health (NIOSH) in the United States, the Institute of Work, Health and Organizations (I-WHO) at the University of Nottingham under the leadership of Tom Cox, the work of Cary Cooper and his team at the University of Manchester Institute of Science and Technology (UMIST), and the Institute for Work Psychology at the University of Sheffield.

The American Psychological Association and NIOSH invested considerable resources in developing this area of occupational health. Theirs was a three-pronged approach where they sponsored stress conferences, founded the *Journal of Occupational Health Psychology* and gave grants to a number of universities to establish occupational health psychology training. Those involved in these efforts included Steve Sauter and Lois Tetrick. The fundamental change in terms of occupational health, argue Barling and Griffiths, is that whereas at the beginning of the twentieth century work was primarily organized around the goals of management "increasingly we are witnessing a desire to promote and protect the psychological and physical health of workers themselves" (2003, p.30).

Post-Traumatic Stress Disorder

Stress reactions to "traumatic incidents, complex as they are, can be understood essentially as the reactions of normal human beings to sudden, unexpected and terrifying events in their lives" (Hodgkinson and Stewart, 1991, p.10). Post Traumatic Stress Disorder (PTSD) grew out of the work in many fields of trauma stress, and is recognized as a long-standing and pervasive disorder. While not unique to war its identification as a separate diagnostic category is sometimes traced to two unusual features of the Vietnam War (Healy, 1993). These features were the awareness of the public to what was going on at the battle-front and the nonacceptance of the war itself. "This more than anything else," argued Healy "led to an atmosphere in which the difficulties that returning veterans were having were made salient. It led to the official recognition of a post-traumatic stress syndrome" (1993, p.105). PSTD was first outlined in 1980 in the third edition of the *Diagnostic and Statistical Manual of Mental Disorders* of the American Psychiatric Association (DSM-III).

The DSM-III described the symptoms following the experience of an event "outside the range of usual human experience and that would be markedly distressing to almost anyone" (Hodgkinson and Stewart, 1991, p.11). Initially the event was described in terms of a combat or hostage situation or a natural disaster but PSTD, as Healy suggests, "has rapidly broken through these restriction" (1993, p.105) to include events such as bereavement, business loss, or other terrifying or horrible situation. The symptoms include (see Healy, 1993; Hodgkinson and Stewart, 1991) re-experiencing the trauma, a numbing of general responsiveness, and symptoms of increased arousal. Models of post-traumatic stress reactions which begin with the traumatic event and worked their way via intrusive memories and establishing meaning to emotional arousal and avoidance behaviors offered opportunities for developing intervention strategies. Much of the PSTD research literature now focuses on reviewing, describing, and evaluating the benefits and constraints associated with the application of such interventions as trauma debriefing programs, post-trauma defusing, pre-trauma education and training, and traditional counseling.

Summary

Since research into stress at work first began to appear in the 1950s and 1960s it has become a field of endeavor that has found its way into every facet of working life and beyond. There is no reason to suspect that the volume of research is likely to decrease. The field has passed through numerous phases that have captured the imagination and creativity of researchers. But just as there is a sense that work stress research has now reached a level of maturity there is still a lingering sense of disquiet about established methods and practices, the theory that surrounds them and what is needed in terms of an organizing concept for the future. What is also apparent is that the maturing of work stress research has provided researchers with a set of experiences for evaluating progress and perhaps more importantly for questioning accepted practice, challenging old interpretation, searching for new meanings, and developing a confidence in exploring, developing, and presenting creative and ecologically sensitive methods that are now beginning to establish themselves as the hallmark of contemporary work stress research.

CHAPTER SIX

What Do We Mean By Stress: From the Past to the Future

Introduction

It may seem strange at this point to be asking the question, "what do we mean by stress." Yet, as the history of stress so far has shown, the interest in, controversy surrounding, and passionately held points of view all keep returning to "what is it that we are talking about?" Couple this with an almost insatiable desire to understand the causes and consequences of work stress and the feeling, by many, that the term itself has been hijacked by the professional, popular, and academic press alike and you have an interesting story in its own right (Lazarus, 1999), and any history is a history of good stories. Now, as we get to the end of our historical journey we may be better able to understand why the debate surrounding the term continues and what may be the way forward. The study of stress has been plagued by the confusing use of the term (Lazarus, 1993), to the extent that there are "clearly wide variations in specific uses, specific definitions, and specific purposes for which the term stress has been associated" (Appley and Trumbull, 1967, pp.5–6).

What Do We Mean By Stress?

The debate over the term "stress" has been intense, and there is in stress research almost a tradition to remark on this fact and to query whether stress is any different from simply being alive. Yet from the undercurrents of this debate over the meaning of stress, emerge a number of themes that help to understand why the debate continues and what it is that researchers are looking for and trying to achieve. If "durability provides a good index of the validity or usefulness of scientific concepts" then as already suggested "a continuing search for what is solid and valid" (Mason, 1975a, p.6) in the term must continue.

One of the themes to emerge suggests that accompanying the widespread inconsistency in the use of the term is an inadequate concern for its meaning. This concern stems partly from the way stress has traditionally been defined as a "stimulus," a "response," or an "interaction" between the two, raising the issue of whether each definition tied in some sense to a particular discipline can be easily extended from one discipline to another (Kasl, 1978). And also partly from whether researchers have been excessively "indulgent in a neologic cornucopia and the exuberant use of arbitrary nomenclature" (Haward, 1960, p.187), which has fast become neither precise or consistent – even among those using the same term – resulting in a label that has become progressively more descriptive than explanatory (Ader, 1980). Researchers may have to accept some responsibility for the latter concern, as the term has been allowed to assume an elasticity of meaning with its use being continually extended "to a huge and diverse array of phenomena" (Bartlett, 1998, p.36). It is no wonder that an "antistress movement" has emerged challenging the worth and value of a term that has become to them (e.g. Ader, 1980; Briner, 1994) so confused, to be almost meaningless. Although rather than being antistress, these writers are probably more "anti" the expectation that it is possible to have one term that fits all kinds of diverse explanations. The continuing search for meaning and the intensity that still surrounds the debate simply reflects for most researchers the dictum set down by Wolff in 1953 that if stress "is to enter the language of biological science then responsibilities concerning its meaning are entailed" (p.v). Another theme to emerge from the debate is whether the term stress "which was so fruitful in its time" now "provides an adequate description of the data that are now available to us" (Hinkle, 1973, pp.31–2). Two issues are involved. The first issue is whether current representations of stress actually capture the nature of the experience (Newton, 1995). In other words, to try and resolve this issue and reconcile the reality of stress with its rhetoric, researchers should be constantly asking themselves not so much "why they believe in the *reality* of stress as why [they] believe in current *representations* of stress (Newton, 1995, p.10).

The second issue involves whether greater use of a "discursive perspective" – "one that emphasizes the need to take account of the individual's own experience" (Bartlett, 1998, p.15) – provides the way forward in ensuring that when it comes to defining stress, relevance is seen as just as much a powerful criteria as academic rigor.

A third theme to emerge concerns just how possible it is to transfer meanings of stress from one discipline to another. It is Newton (1995) who points out that it is more difficult to neatly define psychological stress, because of the diversity of interpretive influences, than stress defined in a biological or physiological sense. In a not dissimilar sense, Abbott (2001) talks about the "process of ingestion," where social scientists don't want to let anything go in their search for comprehensiveness – taking in more than they can digest with the result that, because they can never stay within the limits of their own discipline, they are, at the very least, "forced to take up the conceptual and empirical problems of work they displace" (2001, p.59). Yet while acknowledging these difficulties, most stress researchers would, on the one hand, agree that the concept of stress is by its very nature interdisciplinary and, therefore, more collaboration between disciplines is necessary if the concept of stress is to be better understood, but, on the other hand, appear to be quite happy to work quite independently of those other "disciplines which are so essential to a full understanding of the problem" (Bartlett, 1998, p.37). Integration if it is to be successful must, it seems, either come up with an answer to the question of "how do you integrate within a single concept such a wide array of phenomena or search for what is the very essence of the experience and unify different phenomena," around that meaning.

The difficulties encountered in trying to define stress and the lack of any agreement should not be seen as indicative of a definitional crises but "the absence of consensus more properly reflects the rapid expansion of stress research in many divergent directions and may be more conducive to future theorizing than a premature closure" (Breznitz and Goldberger, 1982, p.4). More complex ideas, suggested Paterson and Neufeld (1989, p.9), have "somewhat vague boundaries and attempting to define them gives one a sense of arbitrariness." It seems wise, as Lazarus (1966) points out, to use "stress" as a general term for the whole area of study. The utility of this idea is that it shifts the focus away from regarding stress as a variable to understanding stress as "a rubric consisting of many variables and processes" (Lazarus and Folkman, 1984, p.12). Lazarus goes on to talk about stress as an organizing concept, where the meaning of the word would act as a mechanism for better organizing and understanding a range of phenomena. So rather than trying to bring together a whole range of different phenomena, the focus shifts towards identifying what it is about stress that has "sufficient logic and emotional resonance to yield systematic theoretical and research inquiry that will make a lasting solution" (Liddle, 1994, p.167). One such concept that has the potential to unify the field is the concept of *emotions*. If stress research is, in fact, a study of emotions, then recognizing emotions as the "superordinate" concept may provide the focus that is needed and the pathway that may best link together the process of stress itself (Lazarus, 1999). Considering emotions in terms of their organizing ability will provide an opportunity to evaluate whether they fulfill a "positive rather then an inhibitory purpose and that they are worthy of the intellectual resources focused on them" (Kaplan, 1996, p.374). Our story to date may have brought us closer to understanding the experience of stress and, perhaps, a way forward, and what better way to have done it than through a historical account of the concept itself.

From the Past to the Future

Know your history! This is the message if we are to fully understand and appreciate how the concept of stress has, in a relatively short time "all but pre-empted a field previously shared by a number of other concepts" (Cofer and Appley, 1964, p.441). A good researcher knows "that the history of his [*sic*] subject makes a difference" (Trumbull and Appley, 1967, p.401) and, as Lazarus (1999) suggests, it is important to have a good understanding of the past. Like most histories, the history of stress is, as we now know, one which is full of confusion and controversy (Selye, 1975), of intense debates and disputes, of hints of "disciplinary provincialism" (Levine and Scotch, 1970), on the one hand, and integration attempts that produce nothing but a "a monster" (Singer and Davidson, 1986, p.58), on the other; of terminology so ill defined that researchers engage "in a careless discourse" moving "cavalierly from one level of data to another" (Levine and Scotch, 1970, p.9) and definitions so bewildering in scope that the stress literature "steadily becomes less and less clear about what sort of experiences are not stressful" (Abbott, 2001, p.51).

Yet despite this confusion and controversy there is, running through the history on stress, a rich seam of determination, vision, and discovery that has produced "an aura of academic excitement" (Mason, 1971, p.323); of historical shifts of great moment, of researchers whose work has become other researchers greatest inspiration, and of a term that not only has provided "the field with a searchlight for uncovering and systematizing diverse data" (Levine and Scotch, 1970, p.290) but more importantly provided "a bridge linking many different areas" to provide a more comprehensive understanding of human adaptation and as such making "it one of the most important constructs in the clinical and social sciences today" (Aldwin, 2000. p.20). But what of the future? How can the past inform the future? We believe that there are four themes that we take forward into the future. These are briefly outlined below.

How Does History Add to Our Understanding of Stress?

There are a number of ways in which a historical perspective deepens our understanding. These ways, drawn from the work of a number of authors (Bartlett, 1998; Hergenhahn, 1992; Viney, 1993) are summarized under two not mutually exclusive headings: *contextual* and *developmental* reasons. Under the heading of *contextual reasons* history provides a mechanism for anchoring why different issues emerge, how context and culture both influence and are influenced by research, and why different issues become important. Without this perspective, the present becomes less understood, frequently assumes a disproportionate significance, and limits the motivation to monitor and evaluate contemporary trends, ideas, and debate. History helps to show that knowledge does not, as is sometimes portrayed, accumulate in an almost linear rational fashion, with one idea neatly building on another. In much the same way, a knowledge of history helps to avoid thinking that progress in the field is best represented by "uncovering the 'true' nature of stress and building upon the already substantial collection of 'facts' that have been 'discovered' (Bartlett, 1998, p.23) logically, uncritically, and without confusion, controversy, and intense debate. In short, without a historical perspective we fail to adequately examine "our own assumptions" and lack the basis to "help us keep our thinking straight" (Viney, 1993, p.3).

Developmental reasons build on the above, for without a knowledge of history we must take on faith the importance of different ideas without understanding why we must or where they came from. History informs our perspective making us less likely to be caught by the influences of fads and fashion. History provides both a source of ideas and an understanding of why certain ideas may be more acceptable at one time than another. History also provides a way of satisfying our curiosity, teaching humility, avoiding past mistakes, and providing us with a "healthy skepticism" that "may temper the human tendency to worship methodological or even substantive idols" (Viney, 1993, p.2). Most of all, history gives us a knowledge sometimes humbling, sometimes frustrating but always exciting when we realize that many of the issues currently studied have "been shared and contributed to by some of the greatest minds" (Hergenhahn, 1992, p.3).

Searching for the Organizing Concept of the Future

One more time – what is the concept that researchers can organize around and that will provide the basis on which to build our theory of stress? There is no doubt that the study of stress has been beleaguered by the bewildering use of the term (Lazarus 1993): it is now such a part of our everyday vocabulary, and so much a part of our everyday lives, that it is difficult at times to know whether what is being discussed is a scientific reality or a culturally manufactured concept that has become a "social fact" (Pollock, 1988, p.381). Yet in spite of "almost chaotic disagreement over its definition" (Mason, 1975a, p.6), the term has enduring scientific, popular, and intuitive appeal instilling in many researchers a deep sense that continuing to search for what is concrete and valid in the term will eventually be rewarding (Mason, 1975); an acknowledgment that the fertility of the term greatly outweighs its obvious disabilities (Abbott, 2001). What our history tells us is that search, and that concreteness may, as already discussed, come by focusing on the concept of emotions. It is *emotions* that may give us the organizing concept of the future.

Distinguishing between Description and Meaning

If nothing more, our history has taught us that a history of stress is a history of methodology. Throughout our narrative there are the underlying questions of "where are current methodologies taking us" and "what can alternative methodologies provide." Now more than at any other time, as our understanding of the stress process develops, there is a need to engage in a period of quiet reflection, where we consider how appropriate traditional measurements are in capturing the richness and complexity of that process and to ask "whose reality are we measuring." Now is the time to confront issues like, for example, whether our unquestioning acceptance on reliability has been, at times, at the expense of relevance. Time and time again, writers on stress point to the difficulties surrounding self-report and cross-sectional data, calling for the use of more ecologically sensitive daily processing methods that allow individuals to express how they think and they feel. However, in what seems like an uncontrollable compulsion to move things along this message gets lost. Researchers continue to attach significance to accepted practices without asking "are our measures measuring what we think they are?" The call is not to replace one method with another but to consider how methodological pluralism may provide a way of understanding those processes that link the individual to the environment.

As much can be gained by looking at how traditional measures can be refined to capture the essence of what it is we are trying to measure, as can be gained by exploring the use of different techniques that allow a reality to emerge rather than being imposed. By considering the difference between describing a relationship and giving it meaning, perhaps we will move closer to understanding how appropriate our measures really are. Methods that capture "meaning," are substantively different from those that "describe" relationships. Both description and meaning should be part of all researchers repertoires. The issue, we would argue, is not to be mislead by thinking that by describing a relationship we are in fact giving it meaning.

Why Study Stress? Fulfilling Our Moral Responsibility

If there has been so much controversy surrounding the term stress then why study it? One reason that has been given for studying stress is its "cost" to individuals, communities, organizations, and economies. The cost to individuals has been expressed in terms of the impact of stress on health and well-being, on the quality of life and working life (Kompier and Cooper, 1999), on work-life balance, and on the fact that lifestyles are simply more stressful with people perceiving themselves to be under ever increasing amounts of stress (Charlesworth, 1996). Researchers are, not surprisingly, quick to point out the difficulties involved in assessing the extent of stress-related illness (Jones and Bright, 2001), particularly when it comes to asking just exactly what is being measured when the term stress is used, and whether the increase in stress-related illness is in part due to the popular usage of the term leading to a raised awareness of its potential impact (Pollock, 1988). Nevertheless, evidence continues to accumulate and be reported in terms of the millions of dollars lost each year in production, sickness absence, premature death, and retirements, escalating health insurance costs, the increasing use of stress management interventions, and the wide range of health and well-being issues reported under the banner of stress. How much this evidence is culturally contaminated, filtered as it may be through the belief that life is more stressful anyway and providing the platform for more stress to be reported (Pollock, 1988), should not be ignored. But the volume of published stress research and the questions that still need to be answered "provides good reason as to why it should be necessary to further study the phenomenon of stress" (Bartlett, 1998, p.3).

Over the years the concept of "stress" has been at the center of so much research, and even though it has become an almost essential part of our vocabulary, it has, despite the controversy and confusion, significantly contributed to a changing view as to the way illness is understood (Hinkle, 1973). The idea of single cause single illness has long given way to the now generally agreed belief that the adaptive abilities of individuals and the manner in which they transact with the environment they live in are important causes of illness. So another reason for studying stress is that it brings us closer to understanding how illness is caused and the adaptive processes that individuals engage in. If we are to intervene in that process, then we have a responsibility to better understand the nature of those transactions and the role of stress in causing illness (Bartlett, 1998). Allied to this, is another reason for studying stress, is that the better our understanding of the stress process, the greater the probability that intervention strategies will help to significantly reduce the "human suffering associated with ill health" (Bartlett, 1998, p.3).

Summary

The best way to summarize the reasons discussed above is to make explicit what we think is the underlying theme running through them; that is the most important reason for studying stress is that we have a moral responsibility to those whose lives we research. If stress is an important factor in illness today, then society should expect "those who know something about its antecedents and its mediators to do something about it" (Hamilton, 1979, p.3). Our duty as researchers because of the privileged opportunities we have been given "to study society brings with it the responsibility to better the human condition" (Brief and Cortina, 2000, p.1). To do this we not only have to be committed to contributing to those whose lives we study but ready to assume the responsibility of guaranteeing that our research is ethically based, our methods contribute to the advance of knowledge and understanding, and that our knowledge is being appropriately disseminated to and utilized by policy makers, practioners, and organizations.

The practical application of research ethics, involves evaluating our competence to do research and ensuring that issues of informed consent, confidentiality and anonymity, participant support, protection and rights, and the use of results are all central parts of the research process (see Aguinis and Henle,

2001). The role of ethics also extends to reviewing why we ask the research questions that we do ensuring that by meeting the needs of one group we are not failing in our responsibilities to another. Why, for example are the "implications for managerial practice" so often discussed "but implications for public policies promoting human welfare are seen rarely" (Brief and Cortina, 2000, p.4). Research ethics also extend not just to the way we write up our research but beyond to what Lazarus (1999) describes as "methodological preciousness" where the debate about methods has been dominated by views outlining what some consider to be the proper (or even the only) way of science, inevitably leading to a methodological narrowness that has failed to comprehend our responsibility to think anew about what it is we want to achieve and how best to get there. Unless we accept these responsibilities we will add to the constraints that inhibit the effective utilization of our collective knowledge and simply widen the gap between what it is we are researching and what it is that is relevant to the daily lives of those we research.

References

Abbott, A. 2001: *Chaos of Disciplines*. Chicago: The University of Chicago Press.

Ader, R. 1980: Psychosomatic and psychoimmunological research. *Psychosomatic Medicine*, 42, 307–21.

Aguinis, H., and Henle, C.A. 2001: Conducting ethical research: Much more than a good idea. *The Academy of Management Research Methods Divisional Newsletter* 16, 1–4; 13; 17–18.

Aldwin, C.M. 2000: *Stress, Coping, and Development: An Integrative Perspective*. New York: The Guilford Press.

Appley, M.H., and Trumbull, R. 1967: On the concept of psychological stress. In M.H. Appley and R. Trumbull (eds), *Psychological Stress: Issues in Research*, New York: Appleton-Century-Crofts, 1–13.

Appley, M.H., and Trumbull, R. 1986: Development of the stress concept. In M.H. Appley and R. Trumbull (eds), *Dynamics of Stress: Physiological, Psychological and Social Perspectives*, New York: Plenum Press, 3–18.

Arnetz, B. 2002: Organizational stress. In R. Ekman and B. Arnetz (eds), *Stress; Molecules, Individuals, Organization, Society*. Stockholm: Liber.

Arnold, M.B. 1960: *Emotion and Personality: Vol. I Psychological Aspects*. New York: Columbia University Press.

Bartlett, D. 1998: *Stress: Perspectives and Processes*. Buckingham: Open University Press.

Barling, J., and Griffiths, A. 2003: A history of occupational health psychology. In J.C. Quick and L.E. Tetrick (eds), *Handbook of Occupational Health Psychology*, Washington, DC: American Psychological Association, 19–33.

Barling, J., Kelloway, E.K., and Cheung, D. 1996: Time management and achievement striving interact to predict car sales performance. *Journal of Applied Psychology*, 81, 821–6.

Barone, D.F. 1991: Developing a transactional psychology of work stress. In P.L. Perrewe (ed.), *Handbook on job stress*. [Special Issue] *Journal of Social Behavior and Personality*, 6, 31–8.

Beehr, T.A. 1995: *Psychological Stress in the Workplace*. London: Routledge.

Beehr, T.A. 1998: Research on occupational stress: An unfinished enterprise. *Personnel Psychology*, 51, 835–44.

Beehr, T.A., and Franz, T.M. 1987: The current debate about the meaning of job stress. In J.M Ivancevich and D.C. Ganster (eds), *Job Stress: From Theory to Suggestion*, New York: The Haworth Press, 5–18.

Beehr, T.A., and Newman, J.E. 1978: Job stress, employee health, and organizational effectiveness: A facet analysis, model, and literature review. *Personnel Psychology*, 31, 665–99.

Beehr, T.A., Walsh, J.T., and Taber, T.D. 1976: Relationship of stress to individually and organizationally valued states: Higher order needs as a moderator. *Journal of Applied Psychology*, 61, 41–7.

Ben-Porath, Y.S., and Tellegen, A. 1990: A place for traits in stress research. *Psychological Inquiry*, 1, 14–17.

Blundell, J. 1975: *Physiological Psychology*. London: Methuen.

Booth-Kewley, S., and Friedman, H.S. 1987: Psychological predictors of heart disease: A quantitative review. *Psychological Bulletin*, 101, 343–62.

Breznitz, S., and Goldberger, L. 1982: Stress research at the crossroads. In L. Goldberger and S. Breznitz (eds), *Handbook of Stress: Theoretical and Clinical Aspects*, New York: The Free Press, 3–6.

Brief, A., and Atieh, J.M. 1987: Studying job stress: Are we making mountains out of molehills? *Journal of Occupational Behaviour*, 8, 115–26.

Brief, A., and Cortina, J. 2000: Research ethics: A place to begin. *The Academy of Management Research Methods Divisional Newsletter* 15, 1; 4; 11–12.

Brief, A., and George, J.M. 1991: Psychological stress and the workplace. In P.L. Perrewe (ed.), Handbook on job stress. [Special Issue] *Journal of Social Behavior and Personality*, 6, 15–20.

Briner, R.B. 1994: *Stress: The creation of a Modern Myth*. Paper presented at the Annual Conference of the British Psychological Society, Brighton, March.

Briner, R.B. 1995: *The Experience and Expression of Emotions at Work*. Paper presented at the 1995 British Psychological Society Occupational Psychology Conference, Warwick, UK.

Briner, R.B. 1997: Improving stress assessment: Toward an evidence-based approach to organizational stress interventions. *Journal of Psychosomatic Research*, 43, 61–71.

Brown, G.W. 1990: What about the real world? Hassles and Richard Lazarus. *Psychological Inquiry*, 1, 19–22.

Brown, G.W., and Harris, T.O. 1986: Establishing causal links: The Bedford College studies of depression. In H. Katsching (ed.), *Life Events and Psychiatric Disorders*, Cambridge, England: Cambridge University Press, 107–87.

Burke, R.J. 1971: Are you fed up with work? *Personnel Administration*, 34, 27–31.

Burke, R.J., and Belcourt, M.L. 1974: Managerial role stress and coping responses. *Journal of Business Administration*, 5, 55–68.

Cannon, W.B. 1914: The interrelations of emotions as suggested by recent physiological researchers. *American Journal of Psychology*, 25, 256–82.

Cannon, W.B. 1920: *Bodily changes in Pain, Hunger, Fear and Rage*. New York: D. Appleton and Co.

Cannon, W.B. 1928: The mechanism of emotional disturbance of bodily functions. *New England Journal of Medicine*, 198, 877–84.

Cannon, W.B. 1935: Stresses and strain of homeostasis. *The American Journal of the Medical Sciences*, 189, 1–14.

Cannon, W.B. 1939: *The Wisdom of the Body*. New York: W.W. Norton and Co Inc.

Caplan, R.D. 1983: Person-environment fit: Past, present, and future. In C.L. Cooper (ed.), *Stress Research: Issues for the Eighties*, Chichester: John Wiley and Sons, 35–78.

Cassidy, T. 1999: *Stress, Cognition and Health*. London: Routledge.

Charlesworth, K. 1996: *Are Managers under Stress?* London: Institute of Management.

Chesney, M.A., and Rosenman, R.H. 1980: Type A behaviour in the work setting. In C.L. Cooper and R Payne (eds), *Current Concerns in Occupational Stress*, Chichester: John Wiley and Sons, 187–212.

Cofer, C.N., and Appley, M.H. 1964: *Motivation: Theory and Research*. New York: John Wiley and Sons.

Cohen, S., and Herbert, T.B. 1996: Health psychology: Psychological factors and physical disease from the perspective of human psychoneuroimmunology. *Annual Review of Psychology*, 47, 113–42.

Cohen, F., and Lazarus, R.S. 1973: Active coping processes, coping dispositions and recovery from surgery. *Psychosomatic Medicine*, 41, 109–18.

Cooper, C.L. (ed.) 1998: *Theories of Organizational Stress*. Oxford: Oxford University Press.

Cooper, C.L., and Cartwright, S. 1994: Healthy mind, healthy organization – A proactive approach to occupational stress. *Human Relations*, 47, 455–71.

Cooper, C.L., Dewe, P., and O'Driscoll. M. 2001: *Organizational Stress: A Review and Critique of Theory, Research and Applications*. Thousand Oak, California: Sage.

Cooper, C.L., and Marshall, J. 1976: Occupational sources of stress: A review of the literature relating to coronary heart disease and mental ill health. *Journal of Occupational Psychology*, 49, 11–28.

Cooper, C.L., and Payne, R. 1991: Introduction. In C.L. Cooper and R. Payne (eds), *Personality and Stress: Individual Differences in the Stress Process*. Chichester: John Wiley, 1–4.

Cooper, C.L., Sloan S.J., and Williams, S. 1988: *Occupational Stress Indicator: Management Guide*. Windsor: NFER–Nelson.

Cooper, L., and Bright, J. 2001: Individual differences in reactions to stress. In F. Jones and J. Bright. *Stress: Myth, Theory and Research*. Harlow, England: Prentice-Hall, 111–32.

Costa, P.T., and McCrae, R.R. 1990: Personality: Another "hidden factor" in stress research. *Psychological Inquiry*, 1, 22–4.

Coyne, J.C. 1997: Improving coping research: Raze the slum before any more building. *Journal of Health Psychology*, 2, 153–5.

Coyne, J.C., and Gotttlieb, B.H. 1996: The measure of coping by checklist. *Journal of Personality*, 64, 959–91.

Cox, T. 1978: *Stress*. London: The Macmillan Press.

Cox, T. 1987: Stress, coping and problem solving. *Work & Stress*, 1, 5–14.

Cox, T., and Ferguson, E. 1991: Individual differences, stress and coping. In C.L. Cooper and R. Payne (eds), *Personality and Stress: Individual Differences in the Stress Process*, Chichester: John Wiley and Sons, 7–30.

Cox, T., and Mackay, C. 1981: A transactional approach to occupational stress. In E.N. Corlett and J. Richardson (eds), *Stress, Work Design and Productivity*. New York: John Wiley and Sons, 91–115.

Cummings, T.G., and Cooper, C.L. 1979: A cybernetic framework for studying occupational stress. *Human Relations*, 5, 395–418.

Daniels, K. 1996: Why aren't managers concerned about occupational stress? *Work & Stress*, 10, 352–66.

Daniels, K. 2001: "Stress and emotions: a new synthesis" – a book review. *Human Relations*, 55, 792–803.

DeFrank, R.S. 1988: Psychometric measurement of occupational stress: Current concerns and future directions. In J.J. Hurrell, L.R. Murphy, S.L. Sauter, and C.L. Cooper (eds), *Occupational Stress: Issues and Developments in Research*. New York: Taylor and Francis, 54–65.

DeLongis, A., Folkman, S., and Lazarus, R.S. 1988: The impact of daily stress on health and mood: Psychological social resources as mediators. *Journal of Personality and Social Psychology*, 54, 486–95.

Deutsch, F. 1986: Calling a freeze on "stress wars": There is hope for adaptational outcomes. *American Psychologist*, 41, 713.

Dewe, P. 2000: Methods of coping with stress at work: a review and critique. In P. Dewe, M. Leiter, and T.Cox. (eds), *Coping, Health and Organizations*, London: Taylor and Francis, 3–28.

Dewe, P. 2001: Work stress, coping and well-being: Implementing strategies to better understand the relationship. In P.L. Perrewe and D. Ganster (eds), *Exploring Theoretical Mechanisms and Perspectives*, Volume 1. Amsterdam: JAI-Elsevier Science, 63–96.

Dewe, P., and Guest, D. 1990: Methods of coping with stress at work: A conceptual analysis and empirical study of measurement issues. *Journal of Organizational Behaviour*, 11, 135–50.

Dohrenwend, B.P. 1979: Stressful life events and psychopathology: Some issues of theory and method. In J.E. Barrett, R.M. Rose, and G.L. Klerman (eds), *Stress and Mental Disorder*. New York: Raven Press, 1–15.

Dohrenwend, B.S., and Dohrenwend, B.P. 1974: *Stressful Life Events: Their Nature and Effects*. New York: John Wiley and Sons Ltd.

Dohrenwend, B.S., and Dohrenwend, B.P. 1974a: A brief introduction to research on stressful life events. In B.S. Dohrenwend and B.P. Dohrenwend (eds), *Stressful Life Events: Their Nature and Effects*. New York: John Wiley and Sons Ltd, 1–6.

Dohrenwend, B.S., Dohrenwend, B.P., Dodson, M., and Shrout, P.E. 1984: Symptoms, hassles, social support and life events: Problems of confounded measures. *Journal of Abnormal Psychology*, 2, 222–30.

Dohrenwend, B.P., and Shrout, P.E. 1985: "Hassles" in the conceptualisation and measurement of life stress variables. *American Psychologist*, 40, 780–5.

Doublet, S. 2000: *The Stress Myth*. Freemans Reach, NSW, Australia: IPSILON Publishing.

Edwards, J.R. 1991: The measurement of type A behavior pattern: An assessment of criterion-oriented validity, content validity, and construct. In C.L. Cooper and R. Payne (eds), *Personality and Stress: Individual Differences in the Stress Process*. Chichester: John Wiley and Sons, 151–80.

Edwards, J.R., and Baglioni, A.J. 1991: Relationship between type A behavior pattern and mental and physical symptoms: A comparison of global and component measures. *Journal of Applied Psychology*, 76, 276–90.

Edwards, J.R., and Cooper, C.L. 1988: Research in stress, coping and health: Theoretical and methodological issues. *Psychological Medicine*, 18, 15–20.

Engel, B.T. 1985: Stress is a noun! No, a verb! No an adjective! In T.M. Field, P.M. McCabe, and N. Schneiderman. *Stress and Coping*. Hillsdale, NJ: Lawrence Erlbaum, 3–12.

Eulberg, J.R., Weekley, J.A., and Bhagat, R.S. 1988: Models of stress in organizational research: A metatheoretical perspective. *Human Relations*, 4, 331–50.

Evans, P., Clow, A., and Hucklebridge, F. 1997: Stress and the immune system. *The Psychologist*, 10, 303–7.

Feldman, D.C., and Brett, J.M. 1983: Coping with new jobs: a comparative study of new hires and job changers. *Academy of Management Journal*, 26, 258–72.

Ferguson, E., and Cox, T. 1997: The functional dimensions of coping scale: Theory, reliability and validity. *British Journal of Health Psychology*, 2, 109–29.

Fisher, C.D., and Gitelson, R. 1983: A meta-analysis of the correlates of role conflict and ambiguity. *Journal of Applied Psychology*, 68, 320–33.

Folkman, S. 1982: An approach to the measurement of coping. *Journal of Occupational Behaviour*, 3, 95–107.

Folkman, S., and Lazarus, R.S. 1980: An analysis of coping in a middle-aged community sample. *Journal of Health and Social Behaviour*, 21, 219–39.

Folkman, S., and Lazarus, R.S. 1985: If it changes it must be a process: Study of emotion and coping during three stages of a college examination. *Journal of Personality and Social Psychology*, 48, 150–70.

Folkman, S., Lazarus, R.S., Dunkel-Schetter, C., DeLongis, A., and Gruen, R.J. 1986: Dynamics of a stressful encounter: cognitive appraisal, coping, and encounter outcomes. *Journal of Personality and Social Psychology*, 50, 992–1003.

Frankenhaeuser, M. 1981: Coping with stress at work. *International Journal of Health Services*, 11.

Frankenhaeuser, M. and Ödman, M. 1983: *Stress: A Part of Life*. Stockholm: Brombergs.

Frankenhaeuser, M. and Johansson, G. 1986: Stress at work: Psychobiological and psychosocial aspects. *International Review of Applied Psychology*, 35.

Frankenhaeuser, M. 1991: The psychophysiology of workload, stress and health: comparison between the sexes. *Annals of Behavioral Medicine*, 4, 197–204.

Frankenhaeuser, M. 1993: *Women, Men and Stress*. Höganäs: Bra Böcker/Wiken.

French, J.P.R., and Kahn, R. 1962: A programmatic approach to studying the industrial environment and mental health. *Journal of Social Issues*, 18, 1–47.

French, J.P.R., Rodgers, W., and Cobb, S. (1974). Adjustment as person-environment fit. In G.V. Coelho, D.A. Hamburg, and J.E. Adams (eds), *Coping and Adaptation*. New York: Basic Books, 316–333.

Frese, M. 1977: *Psychische Störungen bei Arbeitern: Zum Einfluss von Gesellschaftlicher Stellung und Arbeitsplatzmerkmalen*. Salzburg: Müller.

Frese, M., and Zapf, D. 1999: On the importance of the objective environment in stress and attribution theory. Counterpoint to Perrewe and Zellars. *Journal of Organizational Behavior*, 20, 761–5.

Friedman, H.S., and Booth-Kewley, S. 1987: The "disease-prone personality:" A meta-analytic view of the construct. *American Psychologist*, 42, 539–55.

Friedman, M., and Rosenman, R.H. 1959: Association of specific overt behavior pattern with blood and cardiovascular findings. *Journal of the American Medical Association*, 169, 1286–96.

Ganster, D.C. 1987: Type A behavior and occupational stress. In J.M. Ivancevich and D.C. Ganster (eds), *Job Stress: From Theory to Suggestion*. New York: The Haworth Press, 61–84.

Ganster, D.C., Schaubroeck, J., Sime, W., and Mayes, B. 1991: The nomological validity of the type A personality among employed adults. *Journal of Applied Psychology*, 76, 143–68.

Gardell, B. 1971: *Production Technology and Work Satisfaction. A Social Psychological Study of Industrial World*. Stockholm: PA-Rådet.

Gavin, J.F. 1977: Occupational mental health – forces and trends. *Personnel Journal* 56, 198–203.

Gergen, K.J. 1985: The social constructionist movement in modern psychology. *American Psychologist*, 40, 266–75.

Glowinkowski S.P., and Cooper, C.L. 1985: Current issues in organizational stress research. *Bulletin of the British Psychological Society*, 38, 212–16.

Grinker, R.R., and Spiegel, J.P. 1945: *Men Under Stress*. New York: McGraw-Hill.

Hagen, D.Q. 1978: The executive under stress. *Psychiatric Annals*, 8, 49–51.

Hamilton, V. 1979: Human stress and cognition: Problems of definition, analysis and integration. In V. Hamilton, and D.M. Warburton (eds), *Human Stress and Cognition: An Information Processing Approach*. Chichester: John Wiley and Sons, 3–8.

Harris, J.R. 1991: The utility of the transaction approach for occupational stress research. In P.L. Perrewe (ed.), *Handbook on Job Stress*. [Special Issue] Journal of Social Behavior and Personality, 6, 21–9.

Haward, L.R.C. 1960: The subjective meaning of stress. *British Journal of Psychology*, 33, 185–94.

Healy, D. 1993: *Images of Trauma: From Hysteria to Post-Traumatic Stress Disorder*. London: Faber and Faber.

Hearnshaw, L.S. 1964: *A Short History of British Psychology 1840–1940*. London: Methuen and Co. Ltd.

Hearnshaw, L.S. 1987: *The Shaping of Modern Psychology*. London: Routledge and Kegan Paul.

Hergenhahn, B.R. 1992: *An Introduction to the History of Psychology.* Belmont California: Wadsworth Pub. Co.

Hinkle, L.E. 1973: The concept of stress in the biological and social sciences. *Science, Medicine and Man,* 1, 31–48.

Hinkle, L.E. 1977: The concept of "stress" in the biological and social sciences. In Z.J. Lipowski, D.R. Lipsitt, and P.C. Whybrow (eds), *Psychosomatic Medicine: Current Trends and Clinical Applications.* New York: Oxford University Press, 27–49.

Hinkle, L.E. 1987: Stress and disease: The concept after 50 years. *Social Science and Medicine,* 25, 561–6.

Hodgkinson, P.E., and Stewart, M. 1991: *Coping with Catastrophe: A Handbook of Disaster Management.* London: Routledge.

Holmes, T.H., and Masuda, M. 1974: Life change and illness susceptibility. In B.S. Dohrenwend and B.P. Dohrenwend (eds), *Stressful Life Events: Their Nature and Effects.* New York: John Wiley and Sons Ltd, 45–72.

Holmes, T.H., and Rahe, R.H. 1967: The social readjustment scale. *Journal of Psychosomatic Research,* 11, 213–18.

Horowitz, M.J. 1990: Stress, states, and person schemas. *Psychological Inquiry,* 1, 25–6.

House, R.J., and Rizzo, J.R. 1972: Role conflict and ambiguity as critical variables in a model of organizational behavior. *Organizational Behavior and Human Performance,* 7, 467–505.

Howard, J.H., Rechnitzer, P.A., and Cunningham, D.A. 1975: Coping with job tension – effective and ineffective methods. *Public Personnel Management,* 4, 317–26.

Howard, A., and Scott, R.A. 1965: A proposed framework for the analysis of stress in the human organism. *Behavioural Sciences,* 10, 141–60.

Howell, W.C. 1991: Human factors in the workplace. In M.D. Dunnette and L.M. Hough (eds), *Handbook of Industrial and Organizational Psychology,* Volume II, (2nd edn) Palo Alto, California: Consulting Psychologists Press, Inc, 209–69.

Ivancevich, J.M., and Matteson, M.T. 1987: Organizational level stress management interventions: A review and recommendations. In J.M. Ivancevich and D.C. Ganster (eds), *Job Stress: From Theory to Suggestion.* New York: the Haworth Press, 229–48.

Ivancevich, J.M., Matteson, M.T., Freedman, S.M., and Phillips, J.S. 1990: Worksite stress management interventions. *American Psychologist,* 45, 252–61.

Jex, S.M. 1998: *Stress and Job Performance: Theory, Research, and Implications for Managerial Practice.* London: Sage.

Jex, S.M., and Beehr, T.A. 1991: Emerging theoretical and methodological issues in the study of work-related stress. *Research in Personnel and Human Resources Management,* 9, 311–65.

Johnson, J.V. 1986: *The impact of the workplace social support, job demands, and work control under cardiovascular disease in Sweden*. Doctoral dissertation, Johns Hopkins University. Distributed by Department of Psychology, University of Stockholm, Report no. 1–86.

Johnson, M. 1991: Selye's stress and the body in the mind. *Advances, The Journal of Mind-Body Health*, 7, 38–44.

Jones, F., and Bright, J. 2001: *Stress: Myth, Theory and Research*. Harlow, England: Prentice-Hall.

Jones, F., and Kinman, G. 2001: Approaches to studying stress. In F. Jones and J. Bright. *Stress: Myth, Theory and Research*. Harlow, England: Prentice-Hall, 17–45.

Kahn, R.L. 1970: Some propositions towards a researchable conceptualisation of stress. In J.E. McGrath (ed.), *Social and Psychological Factors in Stress*. New York: Holt, Rinehart and Winston, Inc, 97–103.

Kahn, R.L., and Byosiere, P. 1992: Stress in organizations. In M.D. Dunnette and L.M. Hough (eds), *Handbook of Industrial and Organizational Psychology*, Volume III, (2nd edn). Palo Alto, California: Consulting Psychologists Press, Inc, 571–649.

Kahn, R.L. and French, J.P.R. 1962: A summary and some tentative conclusions. *Journal of Social Issues*, 18, 122–7.

Kahn, R.L., Wolfe, D.M., Quinn, R.P., Snoek, J.D., and Rosenthal, R.A. 1964: *Organizational Stress: Studies in Role Conflict and Ambiguity*. New York: John Wiley and Sons Inc.

Kanner, A.D., Coyne, J.C., Schaefer, C., and Lazarus, R.S. 1981: Comparison of two modes of stress measurement: Daily hassles and uplifts versus major life events. *Journal of Behavioral Medicine*, 4, 1–39.

Kaplan, H.B. 1996: Themes, lacunae and directions in research on psychological stress. In H.B. Kaplan (ed.), *Psychosocial Stress: Perspectives on Structure, Theory, Life Courses and Methods*. New York: Academic Press, 369–401.

Karasek, R. 1979: Job demands, job decision latitude and mental strain: Implications for job redesign. *Administrative Science Quarterly*, 24, 285–308.

Karasek, R. and Theorell, T. 1990: *Healthy Work. Stress, Productivity and the Reconstruction of Working Life*. New York: Basic Books.

Kasl, S.V. 1978: Epidemiological contributions to the study of work stress. In C.L. Cooper and R. Payne (eds.), *Stress at Work*. Chichester: John Wiley and Sons, 3–48.

Kiev, A., and Kohn, V. 1979: *Executive Stress*. New York: AMACOM.

King, L.A., and King, D.W. 1990: Role conflict and role ambiguity: A critical assessment of construct validity. *Psychological Bulletin*, 107, 48–64.

Kinicki, A.J., McKee, F.M., and Wade, K.J. 1996: Annual Review, 1991–1995: Occupational health. *Journal of Vocational Behavior*, 49, 190–220.

Kompier, M., and Cooper, C.L. 1999: Introduction: Improving work, health and productivity through stress prevention. In M. Kompier and C.L. Cooper (eds), *Preventing Stress, Improving Productivity*. London: Routledge, 1–8.

Latack, J.C. 1986: Coping with job stress: Measures and future directions for scale development. *Journal of Applied Psychology*, 71, 377–85.

Lazarus, R.S. 1966: *Psychological Stress and the Coping Process*. New York: McGraw-Hill Book Company.

Lazarus, R.S. 1977: Psychological stress and coping in adaptation and illness. In Z.J. Lipowski, D.R. Lipsitt, and P.C. Whybrow (eds), *Psychosomatic Medicine: Current Trends and Clinical Applications*, New York: Oxford University Press, 14–26.

Lazarus, R.S. 1983: Psychological stress and coping in aging. *American Psychologist*, 38, 245–54.

Lazarus, R.S. 1984: On the primacy of cognition. *American Psychologist*, 39, 124–9.

Lazarus, R.S 1984a: Puzzles in the study of daily hassles. *Journal of Behavioral Medicine*, 7, 375–89.

Lazarus, R.S. 1990: Theory based stress measurement. *Psychological Inquiry*, 1, 3–12.

Lazarus, R.S. 1990a: Authors response. *Psychological Inquiry*, 1, 41–51.

Lazarus, R.S. 1991: *Emotion and Adaptation*. New York: Oxford University Press.

Lazarus, R.S. 1991a: Cognition and motivation in emotion. *American Psychologist*, 46, 352–67.

Lazarus, R.S. 1991b: The cognitive-emotion debate: A bit of history. In T. Dalgleish and M. Power (eds), *Handbook of Cognition and Emotion*. Chichester: John Wiley and Sons Ltd, 3–19.

Lazarus, R.S. 1991c: Psychological stress in the workplace. In P.L. Perrewe, (ed.) *Handbook on Job Stress* [Special Issue] Journal of Social Behavior and Personality, 6, 1–13.

Lazarus, R.S. 1993: From psychological stress to the emotions: A history of changing outlooks. *Annual Review of Psychology*, 44, 1–21.

Lazarus, R.S. 1993a: Coping theory and research: Past, present, and future. *Psychosomatic Medicine*, 55, 234–47.

Lazarus, R.S. 1995: Vexing research problems inherent in cognitive-mediational theories of emotions – and some solutions. *Psychological Inquiry*, 6, 183–96.

Lazarus, R.S. 1998: *The Life and Work of an Eminent Psychologist: Autobiography of Richard S. Lazarus*. New York: Springer.

Lazarus, R.S. 1998a: *Fifty Years of the Research And Theory of R.S. Lazarus: An Analysis of Historical and Perennial Issues*. Mahwah, NJ: Lawrence Erlbaum Associates.

Lazarus, R.S 1999: *Stress and Emotion: A New Synthesis*. London: Free Association Books.

Lazarus, R.S. 2000: Toward better research on stress and coping. *American Psychologist*, 55, 665–73.

Lazarus, R.S. 2001: Relational meaning and discrete emotions. In Scherer, K.R., Schorr, A., and Johnstone, T. (eds), *Appraisal Processes in Emotion: Theory, Methods, Research*. Oxford: Oxford University Press, 37–67.

Lazarus, R.S., DeLongis, A., Folkman, S., and Gruen, R. 1985: Stress and adaptational outcomes: The problem of confounded measures. *American Psychologist*, 40, 770–79.

Lazarus, R.S., and Folkman, S. 1984: *Stress, Appraisal and Coping*. New York: Springer.

Lazarus, R.S. and Folkman, S. 1987: Transactional theory and research on emotions and coping. *European Journal of Personality*, 1, 141–69.

Lazarus, R.S., and Launier, R. 1978: Stress-related transactions between person and environment. In L.A. Pervin and M. Lewis (eds), *Perspectives in Interactional Psychology*. New York: Plenum, 287–327.

Leahey, T.H. 1992: *A History of Psychology: Main Currents in Psychological Thought*. Englewood Cliffs NJ: Prentice-Hall.

Le Vay, D.L. 1952: Hans Selye and a unitary conception of disease. *British Journal of the Philosophy of Science*, 3, 157–68.

Levi, L. 1990: *Four Decades of Lennat Levi's Research – A Selection*. Stockholm: Karolinska Institute.

Levi, L. 2002: Stress – an overview: International and public health perspective. In R. Ekman, and B. Arnetz (eds), *Stress: Molecules, Individuals, Organisation, Society*. Stockholm: Liber.

Levine, S., and Scotch, N.A. (eds) 1970: *Social Stress*. Chicago: Aldine Publishing Company.

Liddle, H.A. 1994: Contextualizing resiliency. In M.C. Wong and E.W. Gordon (eds), *Educational Resilience in Inner-city America*. Hillsdale, N.Y.: Earlbaum, 167–77.

Lief, A. 1948: *The Common-sense Psychiatry of Dr Adolf Meyer: Fifty-two Selected Papers Edited, with Biographical Narrative*. New York: McGraw-Hill Book Company Inc.

Lipowski, Z.J. 1977: Psychosomatic medicine: Current trends and clinical applications. In Z.J. Lipowski, D.R. Lipsitt and P.C. Whybrow (eds), *Psychosomatic Medicine: Current Trends and Clinical Applications*. New York: Oxford University Press, xiii–xix.

Lipowski, Z.J. 1977a: Psychosomatic medicine in the seventies: An overview. *American Journal of Psychiatry*, 134, 233–44.

Lipowski, Z.J. 1986a: Psychosomatic medicine: past and present: Part I Historical background. *Canadian Journal of Psychiatry*, 31, 2–7.

Lipowski, Z.J. 1986b: Psychosomatic medicine: past and present: Part II Current State. *Canadian Journal of Psychiatry*, 31, 8–13.

Lipowski, Z.J. 1986c: Psychosomatic medicine: past and present: Part III Current research. *Canadian Journal of Psychiatry*, 31, 14–21.

Love, I.N. 1994: Neurasthenia. *Journal of the American Medical Association*, 271, 1242.

Lundberg, U., Mårdberg, B. and Frankenhaeuser, M. 1994: The total workload of male and female white-collar workers as related to age, occupational level, and number of children. *Scandinavian Journal of Psychology*, 35, 315–27.

Martensen, R.L. 1994: Was neurasthenia a "legitimate morbid entity"? *Journal of the American Medical Association*, 271, 1243.

Martin, R.A. 1984: A critical review of the concept of stress in psychosomatic medicine. *Perspectives in Biology and Medicine*, 27, 443–64.

Mason, J.W. 1971: A re-evaluation of the concept of "non-specificity" in stress theory. *Journal of Psychiatric Research*, 8, 323–53.

Mason, J.W. 1972: Organization of Psychoendocrine Mechanisms: A review and reconsideration In N.S. Greenfield and R.A. Sternbach (eds), *Handbook of Psychophysiology*. New York: Holt, Rinehart and Winston Inc, 3–121.

Mason, J.W. 1975: A historical view of the stress field Part I. *Journal of Human Stress*, 1, 6–12.

Mason, J.W. 1975a: A historical view of the field of stress Part II. *Journal of Human Stress*, 1, 22–36.

McGrath, J.E. (ed) 1970: *Social and Psychological Factors in Stress*. New York: Holt, Rinehart and Winston, Inc.

McGrath, J.E. 1976: Stress and behavior in organizations. In M.D. Dunnette (ed.), *Handbook of Industrial and Organizational Psychology*. l Chicago: Rand McNally, 1351–95.

Meyer, A. 1919: The life chart and the obligation of specifying positive data in psychopathological diagnosis. In *"Contributions to medical and biological research dedicated to Sir William Osler in honour of his seventieth birthday July 12 1919."* By his pupils and co-workers, New York: Paul B. Hoeber, 1128–33.

Meyer, A. 1948: The life chart. In A. Lief (ed.), *The Common-sense Psychiatry of Dr Adolf Meyer: Fifty-two Selected Papers Edited, with Biographical Narrative*, New York: McGraw-Hill Book Company Inc, 418–22.

Monat, A., and Lazarus, R.S. (eds) 1991: *Stress and Coping* (3rd edn). New York: Columbia University Press.

Monroe, S.M. 1983: Major and minor life events as predictors of psychological distress: Further issues and findings. *Journal of Behavioral Medicine*, 6, 189–205.

Munsterberg, H. 1913: *Psychology and Industrial Efficiency*. London: Constable.

Murphy, L.R. 1984: Occupational stress management: A review and appraisal. *Journal of Occupational Psychology*, 57, 1–15.

Murphy, L.R. 1987: A review of organizational stress management research: methodological considerations. In J.M Ivancevich and D.C. Ganster (eds), *Job Stress: From Theory tTo Suggestion*. New York: The Haworth Press, 215–227.

Murphy, L.R. 1988: Workplace interventions for stress reduction and prevention. In C.L. Cooper and R. Payne (eds), *Causes, Coping and Consequences Of Stress At Work*. Chichester: John Wiley and Sons, 301–39.

Murphy, L.R., Hurrell, J.J., Sauter, S.L., and Keita, C.P. (eds) 1995: *Job Stress Interventions*. Washington, DC: American Psychological Association.

Muscio, B. 1974: *Lectures on Industrial Psychology* (2nd edn) Cambridge: Easton Hive Pub Company.

Narayanan, L., Menon, S., and Spector, P.E. 1999: Stress in the workplace: A comparison of gender and occupations. *Journal of Organizational Behavior*, 20, 63–74.

Newman, J.E., and Beehr, T.A. 1979: Personal and organizational strategies for handling job stress: A review of research and opinion. *Personnel Psychology*, 32, 1–43.

Newton, T. 1995: *"Managing" Stress: Emotion and Power at Work*. London: Sage.

Oborne, D.J. 1987: *Ergonomics at Work*. Chichester: John Wiley and Sons.

Parkes, K.R. 1994: Personality and coping as moderators of work stress processes: models methods and measures. *Work and Stress*, 8, 110–29.

Parkinson, B. 2001: Putting appraisal in context. In Scherer, K.R., Schorr, A., and Johnstone, T. (eds), *Appraisal Processes in Emotion: Theory, Methods, Research*, Oxford: Oxford University Press, 173–86.

Parkinson, B., and Manstead, A.S.R. 1992: Appraisal as a cause of emotion. In M.S. Clark (ed.), *Emotion*, London: Sage, 122–49.

Paterson, R.J., and Neufeld, R.W.J. 1989: The stress response and parameters of stressful situations. In R.W.J. Neufeld (ed.), *Advances in the Investigation of Psychological Stress*, New York: John Wiley and Sons, 7–42.

Payne, R. 1988: Individual differences in the study of occupational stress. In C.L. Cooper and R. Payne (eds), *Causes, Coping and Consequences of Stress at Work*. Chichester: John Wiley and Sons, 209–32.

Payne, R., Jick, T.D., and Burke, R.J. 1982: Whither stress research? An agenda for the 1980s. *Journal of Occupational Behaviour*, 3, 131–45.

Pearlin, L.I., and Schooler, C. 1978: The structure of coping. *Journal of Health and Social Behavior*, 19, 2–21.

Perrewe, P.L., and Zellars, K.L. 1999: An examination of attributions and emotions in the transactional approach to the organizational stress process. *Journal of Organizational Behavior*, 20, 739–52.

Pollock, K. 1988: On the nature of social stress: Production of a modern mythology. *Social Science and Medicine*, 26, 381–92.

Quick, J.C., and Quick, J.D. 1979: Reducing stress through preventive medicine. *Human Resource Management*, 18, 15–22.

Quick, J.C., and Quick, J.D. 1984: *Organizational Stress and Preventive Management*. New York: McGraw-Hill Publishing Company.

Quick, J.D., Horn, R.S., and Quick, J.C. 1987: Health consequences of stress. In J.M. Ivancevich and D.C. Ganster (eds), *Job Stress: From Theory to Suggestion*. New York: The Haworth Press, 19–34.

Quick, J.C., Quick, J.D., Nelson, D.L., and Hurrell, J.J. (eds) 1997: *Preventive Stress Management in Organizations*. Washington, DC: American Psychological Association.

Rahe, R.H., Meyer, M., Smith, M., Kjaer, G., and Holmes, T.H. 1964: Social stress and illness onset. *Journal of Psychosomatic Research*, 15, 33–9.

Reber, A.S. 1985: *The Penguin Dictionary of Psychology*. Harmondsworth, England: Penguin Books Ltd, 290.

Rizzo, J.R., House, R.J., and Lirtzman, S.I. 1970: Role conflict and ambiguity in complex organizations. *Administrative Science Quarterly*, 15, 150–63.

Rose, N. 1999: *Governing the Soul: The Shaping of the Private Self*. (2nd edn). London: Free Association Books.

Rosenberg, C.E. 1962: The place of George M Bernard in nineteenth-century psychiatry. *Bulletin of the History of Medicine*, 36, 245–59.

Rosenman, R.H., Friedman, M., Straus, R., Wurm, M., Kositchek, R., Huhn, W., and Werthessen, T. 1964: A predictive study of coronary heart disease. *Journal of the American Medical Association*, 189, 103–10.

Rosenman, R.H., Brand, R.J., Jenkins, D., Friedman, M., Straus, R., and Wurm, M. 1975: Coronary heart disease in the western collaborative group study. *Journal of the American Management Association*, 233, 872–7.

Sales, S.M. 1970: Some effects of role overload and role underload. *Organizational Behavior and Human Performance*, 5, 592–608.

Schaubroeck, J. 1999: Should the subjective be the objective? On studying mental processes, coping behavior, and actual exposure in organizational stress research. *Journal of Organizational Behavior*, 20, 753–60.

Schuler, R.S. 1980: Definition and conceptualisation of stress in organizations. *Organizational Behavior and Human Performance*, 25, 184–215.

Schwartz, L.E. and Stone, A.A. 1993: Coping with daily work problems: Contribution of problem content, appraisals, and person factors. *Work and Stress*, 7, 47–62.

Schwarzer, R., and Schwarzer, C. 1996: A critical survey of coping instruments. In M. Zeidner and N.S. Endler (eds), *Handbook of Coping:*

Theory, Research, Applications. New York: John Wiley and Sons, Inc, 107–32.

Scott, R., and Howard, A. 1970: Models of stress. In S. Levine and N.A. Scotch (eds), *Social Stress*, Chicago: Aldine Publishing Company, 259–78.

Selye, H. 1936: A syndrome produced by diverse nocious agents. *Nature*, 138, 32.

Selye, H. 1952: *The Story of the Adaptational Syndrome (told in the form of informal, illustrated lectures).* Montreal: ACTA, Inc.

Selye, H. 1956: *The Stress of Life.* New York: McGraw-Hill Book Company.

Selye, H. 1973: The evolution of the stress concept. *American Psychologist*, 61, 692–99.

Selye, H. 1975: Confusion and controversy in the stress field. *Journal of Human Stress*, 1, 37–44.

Selye, H. 1976: Forty years of stress research: principal remaining problems and misconceptions. *Canadian Medical Association Journal*, 115, 53–6.

Selye, H. 1976a: *Stress in Health and Disease.* Reading, Mass: Butterworths, Inc.

Selye, H. 1977: *Stress Without Distress.* Sevenoaks: Hodder and Stoughton.

Selye, H. 1979: *The Stress of my Life: A Scientist's Memoirs.* (2nd edn), New York: Van Nostrand and Reinhold Company.

Selye, H. 1979a: The stress concept and some of its implications. In V. Hamilton and D.M. Warburton (eds), *Human Stress and Cognition: An Information Processing Approach.* Chichester: John Wiley, 11–32.

Selye, H. 1979b: Stress, cancer and the mind. In J.Tache, H. Selye, and S.B. Day, (eds), *Cancer, Stress and Death.* New York: Plenum Medical Book Company, 11–19.

Selye, H. 1982: History and present status of the stress concept. In L. Goldberger and S. Breznitz, (eds), *Handbook of Stress: Theoretical and Clinical Aspects.* New York: Free Press, 7–17.

Selye, H. 1983: The stress concept: Past, present and future. In C.L. Cooper (ed.), *Stress Research: Issues for the Eighties.* Chichester: John Wiley and Sons, 1–20.

Selye, H. 1991: History and present status of the stress concept. In A. Monat and R.S. Lazarus (eds), *Stress and Coping*, (3rd edn). New York: Columbia University Press, 21–35.

Selye, H., and McKeown, T. 1935: Studies on the physiology of the maternal placenta in the rat. *Proceedings of the Royal Society, London* [biological], 119, 1–31.

Shalit, B. 1977: Structural ambiguity and limits to coping. *Journal of Human Stress*, 3, 32–45.

Shimmin, S., and Wallis, D. 1994): *Fifty Years of Occupational Psychology in Britain*. Leicester: The British Psychological Society.

Singer, J.E., and Davidson, L.M. 1986: Specificity and stress research. In M.H. Appley and R. Trumbull (eds), *Dynamics of Stress: Physiological, Psychological and Social Perspectives*. New York: Plenum Press, 47–62.

Snyder, C.R., and Dinoff, B.L. 1999: Coping: Where have you been? In C.R. Snyder (ed.), *Coping: The psychology of What Works*. New York: Oxford University Press, 3–19.

Somerfield, M. 1997: The future of coping as we know it. *Journal of Health Psychology*, 2, 173–83.

Somerfield, M.R. and McCrae, R.R. 2000: Stress and coping research: Methodological challenges, theoretical advances and clinical applications. *American Psychologist*, 55, 620–5.

SOU 1976: *Work Environment Law*. Stockholm: Statens Offentliga Utredningar 1976:1.

Spector, P.E., Dwyer, D.J., and Jex, S.M. 1988: Relation of job stressors to affective, health, and performance outcomes: A comparison of multiple data sources. *Journal of Applied Psychology*, 73, 11–19.

Stone, I.A., and Neale, J.M. 1984: New measure of daily coping: development and preliminary results. *Journal of Personality and Social Psychology* 46, 892–906.

Sunderland, V., and Cooper, C.L. 2000: *Strategic Stress Management*. London: Macmillan Books.

Sullivan, M.D. 1990: Reconsidering the wisdom of the body: An epistemological critique of Claude Bernard's concept of the internal environment. *Journal of Medicine and Philosophy*, 15, 493–514.

Suls, J., David, J.P., and Harvey, J.H. 1996: Personality and coping: Three generations of research. *Journal of Personality*, 64, 711–35.

Tache, J. 1979: Stress as a cause of disease. In J.Tache, H. Selye, and S.B. Day, (eds), *Cancer, Stress and Death*. New York: Plenum Medical Book Company, 1–10.

Tennen, H., Affleck, G., Armeli, S., and Carney, M.A. 2000: A daily process approach to coping: Linking theory, research, and practice. *American Psychologist*, 55, 626–36.

Theorell, T. (ed) 1997: Future worklife: Special issue in honour of Lennart Levi. *Scandinavian Journal of Work, Environment, and Health 23, Suppl.4.*

Torrington, D.P., and Cooper, C.L. 1977: The management of stress in organizations and the personnel initiative. *Personnel Review*, 6, 48–54.

Trumbull, R., and Appley, M.H. 1967: Some pervading issues. In M.H. Appley and R. Trumbull (eds), *Psychological Stress: Issues in Research*. New York: Appleton-Century-Crofts, 400–12.

Valentine, E.R. 1982: *Conceptual Issues in Psychology*. London: George Allen and Unwin.

Van Harrison, R. 1978: Person-environment fit and job stress. In C.L. Cooper and R. Payne (eds), *Stress at Work*, Chichester: John Wiley and Sons, 175–205.

Van Sell, M., Brief, A.P., and Schuler, R.S. 1981: Role conflict and role ambiguity: Integration of the literature and directions for future research. *Human Relations*, 34, 43–71.

Viney, W. 1993: *A History of Psychology: Ideas and Context*. Boston: Allyn and Bacon.

Viteles, M.S. 1932: *Industrial Psychology*. New York: W.W. Norton.

Watson, D. 1990: On the dispositional nature of stress measures: Stable and non-specific influences on self-reported hassles. *Psychological Inquiry*, 1, 34–7.

Weber, H., and Laux, L. 1990: Bringing the person back into stress and coping measurement. *Psychological Inquiry*, 1, 37–40.

Wittkower, E.D. 1977: Historical perspective of contemporary psychosomatic medicine. In Z.J. Lipowski, D.R. Lipsitt and P.C. Whybrow (eds), *Psychosomatic Medicine: Current Trends and Clinical Applications*. New York: Oxford University Press, 3–13.

Wolfe, D.M., and Snoek, J.D. 1962: A study of tensions and adjustment under role conflict. *Journal of Social Issues*, 18, 102–21.

Wolff, H.G. 1950: Life stress and bodily disease – A formulation. In H.G. Wolff, S.G. Wolf and C.C. Hare (eds), *Life Stress and Bodily Disease*. New York: Hafner Publishing Company Inc, 1059–94.

Wolff, H.G 1953: *Stress and Disease*. Springfield Ill: Charles G. Thomas.

Wolff, H.G., Wolf, S.G., and Hare, C.C. (eds) 1950: *Life Stress and Bodily Disease*. New York: Hafner Publishing Company Inc.

Wozniak, R.H. 1992: *Mind and Body: Rene Descartes to William James*. Available: http://serendip.brynmawr.edu.

Zander, A., and Quinn, R. 1962: The social environment and mental health: A review of past research at the Institute for Social Research. *Journal of Social Issues*, 18, 48–66.

Zajonc, R.B. 1980: Feeling and thinking: preferences need no inferences. *American Psychologist*, 35, 151–75.

Zajonc, R.B. 1984: On the primacy of Affect. *American Psychologist*, 39, 117–23.

Index